The Bamboo Cross

MISSIONARY CLASSICS

Homer E. Dowdy

    CHRIST'S WITCHDOCTOR

    OUT OF THE JAWS OF THE LION

Frank and Marie Drown

    MISSION TO THE HEAD-HUNTERS

Elisabeth Elliot

    THROUGH GATES OF SPLENDOUR

    SHADOW OF THE ALMIGHTY

    THE SAVAGE MY KINSMAN

Margaret Hayes

    MISSING—BELIEVED KILLED

Russell T. Hitt

    JUNGLE PILOT

    CANNIBAL VALLEY

Bruce E. Porterfield

    COMMANDOS FOR CHRIST

Ethel Emily Wallis

    THE DAYUMA STORY

    TARIRI-MY STORY

The
Bamboo Cross

CHRISTIAN WITNESS
IN THE JUNGLES OF VIET NAM

by Homer E. Dowdy

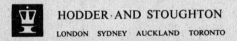

HODDER·AND STOUGHTON
LONDON SYDNEY AUCKLAND TORONTO

Contents

To my wife, Nancy,
as together we've learned
some of these lessons

For ye . . . took joyfully the spoiling of your goods, knowing in yourselves that ye have in heaven a better and an enduring substance.—HEBREWS 10:34

Preface

The world thinks of Viet Nam as a troubled land. In the midst of its war and poverty and disruption have risen heroism and faith and personal victory, and of these the world knows too little. Viet Nam has its Christian stalwarts to match those of any place and time.

That there is a strong, growing, victorious Evangelical Church of Viet Nam is owing almost wholly to the more than fifty years of dedicated effort by the Christian and Missionary Alliance to rear an indigenous body of believers. Encouraged by the founder A. B. Simpson, Robert A. Jaffray crossed from China in 1911 to establish the first Protestant mission in then French Indo-China. From the time of this great missionary pioneer and statesman to the present, the one purpose of the Alliance has been to win the people in full commitment to Jesus Christ.

Not to set up mission schools and orphanages and hospitals, but through teaching of the Bible to establish the Church, believing that a well-taught Church will develop its own conscience for the physical, social, economic, and educational needs of its people—this has been the guiding rule. Though I have mentioned the Christian and Missionary Alliance sparingly in this book, so faithful to the task have its missionaries been that its name might have appeared on almost every page.

When one speaks of Viet Nam, most persons visualize Orientals in picturesque dress who balance heavily loaded *ghan* sticks on their shoulders and who drink tea incessantly and shake hands in natural politeness—and for the most part they are right.

Yet, within Viet Nam are a million or more mountain tribespeople who, though still a part of the Southeast Asian republic, differ in

11

race and culture. The mountainfolk are kin to the people of the South
Pacific, and in many ways resemble the jungle Indians of South
America. Until a few years ago the only name for them was *mois,*
meaning savage, and today in remote areas there are yet unsubdued
tribesmen.

But among the tribes, too, are some of the finest of Christians,
some of the most exemplary ladies and gentlemen of the Far East.
Those whose story is traced here are only a part of the Tribal District
of the Evangelical Church, which also numbers thousands of believers
among the Oriental Vietnamese.

When I went to Viet Nam in 1962, I intended to chronicle the
development of the Vietanamese church and knew there were many
instances of great faith and heroism to document it. I crisscrossed
the country from the Laotian border to the China Sea, from the 17th
Parallel to the Mekong Delta, collecting fascinating material, with the
only problem being its large quantity. Then one day I came across Sau
and Kar and the people whom they had led in soul-searing times.
From their lips I heard their almost incredible but true story, and
knew that in them and in their precious faith I had found the specimen
of all that happened to shape the lives of Christians in this land.

It was my privilege to live in the simple bamboo homes of the very
real people who make up this book, to enjoy their hospitality, to
witness their dependence on God. I am grateful to Sau and Kar and
to La Yoan and Thanh and Doi and to many others for their patience
in putting up with one who strained so hard for the detail of not only
yesterday but of years past.

I spent many days (and long evenings that *seemed* short) in the
home of Herbert and Lydia Jackson, whose obedience to the Lord's
commission of "Go ye" (even to nearly forgotten tribespeople) was
in 1929 the first link of a miraculous chain. From them I caught the
spirit of each unfolding event, be it the attempt at insurrection by
python worshipers or the village revivals in which faith received new
vigor.

Mr. and Mrs. Jean Funé and Mr. and Mrs. George Irwin, all much
loved by the tribesfolk, were of tremendous help. So were the Misses
Peggy Bowen, Evelyn Holiday, and Helen Evans—all of them serving
the Christian and Missionary Alliance. Over her dozen years of ministry
to the tribes Miss Evans has written home faithfully week by week,

and those letters, fortuitously preserved by her mother, made my job easier. Mr. and Mrs. John Newman of Overseas Crusades were of real help in getting to know tribal ways, and Ernest Lee, of Wycliffe Bible Translators, stuck doggedly to the task of interpreting for me.

Homeside, I am grateful to the Rev. Louis L. King, foreign secretary of the Christian and Missionary Alliance, who endorsed this project from the start. I am deeply indebted to one of the best friends a writer ever had, Edward R. Sammis, an exacting critic and tutor throughout the book's progress. To Melvin Arnold, Frank Elliott, and Eleanor Jordan of Harper & Row I owe much, and acknowledge it.

What is produced here is an account of one people's experience in living by faith, even when it had to be done under pressure and peril. I have tried to re-create the developments as they occurred; at times I have paraphrased scenes and speech to bring out the drama and suspense that were inherent.

While writing of these people of Viet Nam I felt again and again that we of another country, another culture, can learn from them. If by my efforts some will, to God (as Sau would say) be the praise.

H. E. D.

The Bamboo Cross

1

A Bent to Shedding Blood

At THE FAR END of the shadowy bamboo longhouse a figure in baggy black trousers and old white shirt lay on the slatted floor.

He was motionless and quiet except for his unnaturally heavy breathing. Nearer the open doorway a half-dozen scantily clad men squatted around a fire that licked up from a clay-bottomed box. Although the men talked darkly about the solitary figure—they called him Sau—they paid him slight attention; from the rhythmic sound of his breathing they thought he was asleep.

In the faint light of the fire none of them could see that under his body Sau clutched the knife at his waist; far from being relaxed, his every muscle was tensed for a sudden, swift spring.

One of those who squatted was an old man with long-flowing silvery hair and a few proudly cultivated whiskers. Around his bony shoulders he wore the bright-colored cloth that marked him as a sorcerer.

"Destroy everything white," the old fellow muttered, loosening his shawl-like covering restlessly. "When the dawn comes the women will destroy everything white in our village—white chickens, white pigs . . . The men . . ." Here he bent forward and lowered his voice to a whisper.

Straining to hear, Sau caught the name "Dalat." Dalat was a provincial capital in the land that was later to be called Viet Nam, two days' walk from this mountain village.

"White!" That meant people in Dalat, too. Sau had friends in Dalat, friends who were missionaries—white missionaries.

As he heard the men around the fire accept with eagerness the command to kill, his heart pumped wildly and a feeling of nausea

B

rose within him. To think that these schemers were his fellow tribesmen!

The air in the murky house had become oppressive. He wished
he were nearer the doorway; he wanted to run from this house and
this village, to run to Dalat to warn his friends that the maddened
men from the mountains would soon be on their way to kill them.

But the plotters were between him and the single opening in the
room. Sau gripped his knife more tightly. He could fight his way
out, he told himself. Since the men thought he was asleep, he would
hold the advantage of surprise. For the moment, he lay quite still,
wondering if he should move. Then the sorcerer spoke again, and
Sau realized that his chance had vanished.

All eyes were suddenly turned on him.

"There in the shadow lies the traitor to our spirits!" the sorcerer
intoned with great emotion.

"He teaches about a sacrifice that's better than the blood of our
animals," added a younger man.

"What could be better than *his* blood?" asked another, and the
speaker laughed at his little joke.

"Nothing could be better than to shed his blood," agreed the
sorcerer grimly. As soon as he had spoken, the suggestion suddenly
ceased to be a joke for any of them.

Sau's blood. That's what they wanted now. The blood of white
men tomorrow—but at this moment they wanted Sau's blood.

"The one who wears the white shirt," a new voice muttered,
"we'll kill him first."

"Before the dawn," put in another.

Quietly, Sau watched them as they fingered their knives. Had
his final hour come? Was he to die at the hand of one who had
been his friend?

Some among them had once begged him to teach them about the
Spirit of the Skies. He did so, and they seemed to be apt and eager
pupils. Yet these same pupils were now plotting to spill his blood.

What had gone wrong? Where had he failed? It did not matter if
they killed him. But if they should kill him before he could warn
the missionaries in Dalat, then who would be left to tell them about
the Spirit of the Skies, the God of Heaven?

It was this prospect that brought desperation to his thoughts.

To his body it brought movement—sudden, swift, explosive action. He leaped to his feet and made a wild dash for the doorway.

Sau did not live in this village, but he had been here so many times that everyone knew him. He always came in black trousers and old white shirt—dressed like the people who lived in towns, not in tribal villages. He stood out in contrast to the mountain men in their loincloths. Yet they had never minded this difference. Also, it never seemed to bother them that what he taught contradicted their age-old tribal beliefs. In Sau they made allowance for these disparities.

Like them, he was brown-skinned, with black eyes and lustrous blue-black hair. But where their hair was straight, his hair lay on his head in short, tight curls. Like them he was expert with the crossbow; he had killed as many tigers as any. Working shoulder to shoulder with them, he had dug deep pits to trap wild elephants for the ivory tusks. Oh, he was stalwart all right—no question. But he was also blessed with good humor. Wherever Sau went among the mountain villages, he talked and people listened. He was inclined to be explosive in his enthusiasm either for or against something; his natural warmth, however, assured him a welcome wherever he went.

Though Sau was young for wisdom—he was then in his early twenties—tribesmen sought him out to settle their quarrels. When sickness struck, they asked him what to do. And they followed his advice on bringing up their children.

Today, however, everything had been different. He arrived in late afternoon. But this time he received no welcome.

Oddly, no men were about, only the grannies who sat clustered in the shade of a house, caring for the few village children.

Sau greeted them as he passed. To his astonishment, they responded by shaking their gnarled fists in his face. At one point they barred his way, thrusting their toothless jaws toward him; apparently in anger, they muttered mysteriously that before long someone was going to die.

He thought at first they must be joking. But there was venom in their raspy voices. It was a threat—a real threat. But against whom was it directed? Surely not against him. He was their friend.

Sau thought about them as he walked on, bound for the home of the village elder. He well knew the persuasive power the old women held in the villages of his people; he also knew how easily they were upset by trifles, carrying on like silly girls. Had he offended one of them perhaps during his last visit? He would find out which one; no doubt the gift of a chicken would appease her.

This decided, he could smile as he reached his destination. The elder's house was one of five thatched, gable-ended dwellings that made up the village, typical of the remote settlements of mountain tribespeople in Southeast Asia. The houses, extending about fifteen double arm-lengths, and perched on legs of short, thick logs, were known as longhouses. Each sheltered an entire clan of about fifty people. There was an uncovered veranda at one end reached by a leaning pole with notches carved in it for steps.

Sau mounted the pole. Before entering the dark interior he turned, almost instinctively.

A hundred paces away, sitting in a circle between two other houses, he saw the men of the village. Silently, obsessively, they were drinking rice alcohol through looping straws of reed from a dozen tall, glazed, green jars.

He called out to them. None looked his way. Surely they must have heard him, but they gave no sign. Even the village elder, usually a genial man—especially when his belly was stretched tight from too much drink—took no notice of him. Sau called again; he asked them to come to him on the elder's veranda. Not one of them so much as raised his head.

They went on drinking. Sau looked about. The scene was eerie. There was no movement, no other sound; just the silent sucking at the jars, the subdued murmuring of the old women, and the cries of the children from somewhere out of sight.

He stood at the doorway, perplexed. Never before had he needed to call out; no sooner would he appear than the village men flocked around him to exchange playful blows and then, this welcome over, to listen to his talk.

But this afternoon he might have been a foreigner wearing foreign clothes, speaking a foreign tongue. Now that he thought of it, even a foreigner, though unwanted, would have been accorded a cordial reception. The tribesmen would feel insulted were a traveler to pass through their village without stopping to eat a meal.

Just then the old sorcerer addressed the tribesmen in a low, almost confidential tone. They listened intently. Their eyes followed him as he rose to his feet and pushed back a faded turban.

The sorcerer looked like one who would consort with the spirits. His small mocking eyes, his leathery face, his garb, all contributed to the aura of mystery that surrounded him.

With one hand he secured the long cloth draped around his shoulders. With the other, he snatched the lid from a battered black kettle beside him, reached in, and lifted out two wriggling baby snakes.

"*Eee-yai!*" The men let out a startled scream.

He held up the mottled reptiles—each no longer than his arm—for all to see.

The reeds bobbed forgotten in the jars as all heads craned forward.

"These are the children of the shining white python!" the sorcerer chanted. He spoke boldly now in the husky, thick tone of one intoxicated. "The serpent has told us to worship her; and she has sent these, her babies, to remind us."

From his vantage point Sau watched. Mountain tribesmen worshiped many strange objects as deities, but never before had he heard of this one. Sau's people killed pythons for food or to trade at the market as medicinal substance. Indeed, without the sorcerer's patronage these baby snakes would already have found their way into someone's cooking vessel.

Why worship a python, he wondered, and a *white* one at that? Sau had heard that there *were* white pythons. But they were rare, and he had never seen one. Nor had he ever spoken to anybody who did. Really, had the sorcerer? If, in fact, the mother was white, her offspring certainly were not. Sau did not believe that these familiarly marked pythons had sprung from an albino. But it did not seem to matter to these simple, undoubting people, so great was the sorcerer's hold on them. In one brief moment, at his word, the baby snakes had become objects to be obeyed without question.

"Worship our parent!" the reptiles seemed to say to them. The fascinated faithful waited only to be told how.

"The python I saw is a jealous woman," the sorcerer was intoning. "She will not bear the sight of white on others, not even on these her own children."

The tribesmen chattered excitedly.

He put the snakes back into the pot and replaced the lid. Then he adjusted the cloth about his shoulders, and raised his hand for silence.

Someone beat a huge old deerskin drum to call the spirits. In cadence to the beat, the sorcerer began to speak in measured, hypnotic tones, telling of his experience.

"Some days ago," he related, "out on the trail I met a stranger. He did not look like anyone I had ever seen. He was a man from far away, a traveling sorcerer from somewhere beyond our own mountains—one more powerful than I. We talked of this and that, then he instructed me to look for a white python.

"The serpent had a message, so the stranger said—a message of death to all that was white. He then hurried off to find other local sorcerers to whom to impart his instructions.

"I obeyed his command," the turbaned man declared to his enraptured audience. "My diligence was soon rewarded.

"Under the house where I store my rice, out in the middle of my field beyond the village, I found the white python coiled about her eggs.

"As I approached, she reared her head. I fell back, frightened, but in the words of our own tongue she ordered me to come close. I crept nearer." The sorcerer's voice fell to a hush; then it rose to a high-pitched, excited whine. "She said to destroy everything white."

Sure enough, the men in the circle murmured; the mysterious traveler had said they would. The drum beat faster as the sorcerer continued:

" 'If you disobey,' the snake said to me—and her beady eyes glared directly into mine—'I will track you down wherever you are —on the trail or in your field or in your house—and I will wrap myself around you and crush you until all your breath is gone.'

"Then," he continued, "to seal the solemnity of her command, before my eyes she hatched two brown-and-yellow babies. These, she said, I must scoop up into a pot and take back to the village.

" 'The sight of them,' she said to me, 'will convince your people that you have talked with me.' "

The sorcerer fell silent. The time had come to let the men, inflamed by the drink, ponder his words.

Several shouted at once, above the beat of the drum:

"Everything white must be destroyed! The python's command!"

"White chickens must die! White goats! Burn the white clothing that some men wear!"

Sau glanced down at his white shirt. Then his gaze shifted uneasily back to the circle.

Once he, too, had sat long at the jar, sensing the tingle that ran up the arms and legs, the fancy that brought reeling pictures to the brain. He noticed that the old one skillfully blended the potency of entrancing words with the headiness of the drink. Sau knew that momentarily the double impact could arouse the villagers to reckless frenzy.

One man stood up, then another, and another. The sorcerer raised his hand to restrain them; he had more to say. But some were already reaching for brass gongs lying close by. Slipping the carrying cords over their shoulders, they added to the thunder of the growling drum the metallic chime of their gongs. All the men were on their feet. They began stomping to the rhythm. Even the sorcerer could not stop what he had started.

"Kill all that's white!" shouted one. Others picked it up. The cry became a chant.

"Spill the blood of the white chicken!" shouted another. Soon the mob chorused ". . . and the blood of the white *man!*"

The sun slipped slowly to the edge of the purple mountains. Sau watched the near-naked figures move from the jars into an open space and become black silhouettes against the fiery orange.

They danced vigorously, kicking out a leg, thrusting forth the head, shaking the whole body in a crude imitation of the suppleness of the python, as they shouted allegiance to their newest deity.

Only after the sun disappeared did they expend themselves, in the brief twilight returning to the jars to suck again on the reeds and give ear once more to the sorcerer.

An albino child—should one be born that night—would, he assured them, be sacrificed to the serpent goddess. In the town of Dalat, at the end of the trail, merchants, officials, soldiers, the white rulers in their big stone houses, all must be destroyed. Also the people of the yellow race. The short, slender men of the cities and

of the flooded level lands appeared pale to the brown-skinned mountaineers; these yellow men had descended from wandering hordes
of the north and never mixed with the tribesmen. The sorcerer was
quick to include them with the hapless white.

Sau swelled with helpless anger. The old fellow was inciting the
villagers to murder! Why, they were even eager to be led along so
horrible a path! He scowled; his temples throbbed.

"There are others . . ." The sorcerer wasn't quite finished. "You
must kill those faithless ones, whether brown like us or white, who
bring the Spirit of the Skies to our hills."

Who was this but Sau? Yet not Sau alone. He thought of others
—of one in particular, a happy, buoyant man who, with his smiling
wife, had come from beyond the seas—a man named Jackson.

It was Jackson who brought to Sau for the first time the news
about the One Good Spirit—the God of Heaven, they called him.

Then one day poor, unschooled Sau, the boy from the mountains,
did more than learn about this Spirit of the Skies. He came to know
Him; and from that moment on his life was changed.

The God of Heaven was new to Sau. His people had been bound
to earth for countless generations. Only in trying daily to appease a
host of hostile spirits, each one dedicated to his hurt and destruction,
was there even a fragile hope of happiness. But from the day he
knew, Sau could look up from the mossy forest floor to the mountain
peaks and above them; up to the clouds and the sun and the stars
and know that his God was greater than all that he saw.

How everlastingly grateful he was for this change! Through his
teachers' love and patient instruction, his life took a new direction, a
new dedication, a new vision.

Someday—how often he dreamed of it, how unflinchingly he
worked for it!—his people would also find release. He had never
doubted that the day would come.

Now, as he listened to these frenzied men who had become wilder
than the animals in the forest, he began to wonder if his dream were
to be destroyed by the very ones for whom he had worked and prayed.

The Jacksons—Grandfather and Grandmother, Sau called them
out of respect—meant only good to the tribesmen. No one else had
shown these forgotten people such love and concern. Leaving their
own country, the two came to this land to speak about God to a
people who didn't much want to know.

Once, long ago, the colonial rulers had arrested Jackson for preaching.

"*Sacré Bleu!*" one government officer growled to another. "That missionary will set these natives to thinking they ought to live like us."

He was quite serious. A few days later the *commissionaire* informed Jackson he was henceforth forbidden to travel in tribal country. So the missionary invited the people who came out of the hills now and then to Dalat's market to build their night fires in his compound and in the light and warmth of them to listen to his teaching.

Sau had told the people of this village all about Grandfather. Some knew him themselves. They were aware that he was a white foreigner, and they knew what he taught. Like all the men taught by Grandfather, Sau wore a white shirt. It had become a sort of symbol adopted by the growing band that took the news of God to the villages where the teacher himself could no longer go.

White-shirted Sau had by now become a familiar figure in the mountains. In village after village he gathered people around him to tell them that the Spirit of the Skies, the God of Heaven, created them, that God loved them, that God's Son had even died in their behalf. They understood the shedding of the Son's blood in sacrifice. Did they not kill their animals in sacrifice for the power of their blood? Yet, just because they understood, they did not necessarily accept. Jesus could become one of their gods, but He had to take His place with the time-honored spirits of the frog and the mountain and the morning dew. Truly to understand would take time.

Here and there a few had turned from appeasing the demons to enjoying a friendship with the God of Heaven. Those in this village had seemed close to turning, and this, no doubt, caused the old sorcerer grave concern. He was shrewd—the sorcerer was—he knew how to fan the smoldering dislike for the foreigners and to join it to his own hatred of a rival belief that, should it prevail, could shunt him and his craft into limbo. He manipulated well their penchant for shedding blood, leading them, through arousing their desire to kill water buffalo and pigs, on to wanting to kill men.

The air fairly crackled with murderous tension.

The village men had ignored Sau when he arrived in the late afternoon, and they seemed to have forgotten his presence now. He knew, though, they would soon remember. Sau had a sudden impulse to flee. But he felt constrained to stay until he knew more of their plans.

Again he saw the men dance, now in the light of a fire someone had started just beyond the houses. And once again the dancing rose to a crescendo of vigorous movement until the tribesmen collapsed.

The fire grew dim. Some men stretched out beside it to sleep. The sorcerer gathered his cloth about his shoulders. He took off his turban and tucked it into his waistcord. A few persons broke the circle to go into their houses.

The revel was over. Sau entered the elder's dark house and felt his way along the jar-lined wall to the end of the room. There he stretched out on the floor. He fingered his knife, drew it out for more comfort, on second thought replaced it in his belt. He settled down, not to sleep, but to pray and watch the night through.

Soon someone mounted the notched pole, bent over the clay-bottomed firebox in the middle of the floor, and blew to life the nearly dead embers. He recognized the elder's wife. Moments later she went out and a handful of men came in, including the village elder and the sorcerer.

For a long while the men sat on the floor by the fire, talking in low tones about the python. They pushed the ends of tree limbs into the fire to keep it ablaze, and also sipped through reeds from a jar that one of them had brought inside. In the sparsely furnished room they could not help but see Sau, but no one gave any sign of knowing or caring that he was there. Sau pretended sleep, although never had he been more alert.

The sorcerer was explaining how the worship of the white python goddess would spread throughout their mountains. This was not the first village to embrace her, he said, nor would it be the last; but he was sure that none had received her so well. Through most of the night he talked, sometimes softly, soothingly, sometimes roughly and with mounting fury. The men paid close heed. Even the women, who had now stolen into the house, sat listening attentively on their straw mats away from the fire.

Midnight was long past when the sorcerer brought the conversation around to Sau. The men at the fire, talking freely because they supposed him asleep, vented their long-restrained anger. They were growing weary of his opposition to their alcohol jars and to the

spirits which they summoned when they had been drinking. Today
they were in no mood to listen to his talk about the Spirit of the
Skies.

Now they spoke of how they would kill Sau.

They had thought that they could dispose of him when they willed.
But the instant Sau sprang toward them they realized they had been
deceived. Before they could scramble to their feet, Sau bounded past
them and was out the doorway, down off the veranda and running.
Stunned, they shrieked curses after the fleeing figure. Then they
stumbled over one another in a clumsy, drunken effort to pursue him.

He was nimbler than they and easily stayed ahead of them. In
the darkness he whipped around a corner, seeking the space between
the houses that led to the trail. Then, across his path, he saw some
of the old grannies who had huddled over the children the evening before. He had run into a nest of them, squatting before the house and
smoking.

He shifted his weight and veered sharply, but not before one old
crone reached out to grasp him. Wouldn't they like to see him
sprawled, a prey for knives and sticks! It had been these hags to
whom the men looked for guidance when first the sorcerer appeared
with his kettle of snakes; it had been these wrinkled old grannies
who nodded to their daughters' husbands as if to say, "Listen well
to the sorcerer." And the men had obeyed.

Sau felt a tug at his shirt, pulling him up short. He struggled for
a moment; then he heard a tearing noise and he was free. He was
running again, leaving them thwarted and angry. Their toothless
gums flapped excitedly as they screamed after him that they had
called for his death—and would see him dead yet!

2

More Piercing than Spears

Sᴀᴜ ᴅɪᴅ ɴᴏᴛ ꜱᴛᴏᴘ ʀᴜɴɴɪɴɢ until he was certain he had outdistanced his pursuers. Then, safe in the depths of the forest, he sat down on the trunk of a fallen tree to catch his breath and collect his thoughts.

What should he do now? Only he, Sau—of all people on earth—could prevent the killings. But how?

He still had a little time. It would take a while for the tribesmen to assemble for their march on Dalat. Some would have to be awakened from their stupor; others would return again for more courage from the alcohol jar.

But there was not *much* time. All too soon the streaks of morning light would come; then the men would gather up their crossbows, their curved-handled shoulder axes, their sticks sharpened into spears, and move out on their errand of murder.

Grandfather was in danger. Sau must go at once to Dalat to warn him.

The village in which Sau lived, Sondianwit—the Village of Sixteen Mountain Peaks—was not far out of his way. Why not, he reasoned, stop there and persuade his younger brother Kar to go with him?

Sau reached home just as dawn broke. He roused his brother from his sleep and explained his predicament. Kar quickly agreed to go with him. Sau stuffed a few things into a bamboo basket. They tarried just long enough to bolt down two bowls of rice. Then before others in the village were stirring, they set out.

Sau had traveled the long trail to Dalat many times, although never with the haste that today's race demanded. The trail was always filled with danger. Tigers might lie in wait, ready to spring, even in day-light hours; also, huge wild humpbacks known as gaur, the black beasts with the massive horns, might charge. But today there was

28

added to the normal hazards the possibility of meeting the frenzied, fanatical killers, thirsting for blood.

The perils were as uncertain as they were great. Only one thing was sure: he had to reach Dalat ahead of the murdering band.

Sau was a few steps in the lead. Short and stocky but with a wiry flex to his frame, he pressed forward down the trail.

Once he had to wait for Kar to catch up. It was not that the younger brother lacked stamina. He had the strength of youth. But to match Sau's vigorous step and the relentless drive that kept him always moving was a feat at any time; to carry a shoulder pack on this arduous trail pushed the lanky Kar almost to his limit.

Kar was not yet twenty; Sau was about four years older. Lively eyes looked out from their frank and friendly faces toughened by sun and wind. Kar's head, like his brother's, was crowned by a mop of bristling curls. Sau wore his torn white shirt. Kar's shirt was a peasant's black, as were his trousers. Kar owned no shoes, and although Sau had a pair with him, they rode in the bamboo basket high on Kar's back.

The faces of the two brothers were a study in contrasts. Sau's bespoke happiness, a keen mind, and a compassionate heart. Kar's bore a touch of mischief; deep in the eyes, however, lurked a shadow —the shadow of haunting fear. Though a follower of Sau in most things, Kar, unlike his brother, still pinned his faith to the spirits of evil.

But on their life-saving mission, Kar was one with Sau.

The two groped their way through mists that enveloped the high mountains. With the help of walking sticks, they slid down shady, steep slopes springy with pine needles. Often they leaped from rock to rock to cross a cascading stream.

Suddenly they burst from the dim forest into the sunlight and face-to-face with a straight stone wall of mountain. It was broken only by a path, which, extending along a narrow shelf, formed the most perilous link in the trail.

With the sureness of experience they pushed along the fingernail ledge, the only way they could pass, hardly breaking step and never pausing to look down the dark ravines.

Finally they reached the end of the ledge. Into the forest they plunged again, driving themselves over rotting logs and tangled roots and around bamboo clusters in the sodden footing of the jungle, grown thicker at this lower altitude.

Darkness would overtake them on the trail. Before they camped tonight they must get as close to Dalat as possible, for Sau was determined to reach there before sunup next day.

"So far, we have seen no sign of the sorcerer and his men," said
Kar, as he and Sau stepped deftly on slimy stones to cross another
stream.

"That is so," Sau nodded, wondering.

The path from the sorcerer's village and that from Sau's Sixteen
Peaks ran parallel for much of the distance to Dalat. A mountain
ridge separated them. Sau had no idea where along their path the
marching villagers might be.

Could the sorcerer's band have started sooner than he thought? If
so, they would be the first to reach the junction of the two paths, and
the first on the main trail to Dalat. Kar and he would have to seek another route if they were to arrive ahead of them.

Still, Sau thought, his brother and he could beat them. Just then it
began to rain.

"We can't make such good time now," he said to Kar.

In minutes the path was slithery mud. They were starting up a
steep incline. For every step forward, they slid back two.

The goal of their race, Dalat—still more than a day away—was a
small but delightful town, the rest and recreation capital of France's
Asian world. To its mild climate, its pine-scented air, its nearby big-
game hunting preserves, came military and civilian personnel on
leave, and planters seeking respite from the humdrum monotony
of their lives.

Comfortable Dalat seemed strangely out of place in the rugged
mountains. And the Frenchmen and Orientals who lived there seemed
even more out of place, surrounded as they were by people so different from themselves.

Sau and Kar belonged to the million or more primitive tribesfolk
who lived in these wild, wooded mountain ranges that spread like
bony fingers down to the South China Sea. The whole peninsula at
this time of 1937 was known as French Indo-China.

The forebears of these mountain people were neither from India
nor from China; they were rather like the islanders, Polynesian, from
the South Pacific. They had come to this mainland three thousand

years before. Here they enjoyed the fruits of the rich river deltas until waves of the yellow race swept down from the north and pushed the brown men from the river valleys and the coastal plain back up into the mountains.

Throughout the millenniums new conquerors arrived periodically to subdue the old. The land became known as Annam, "Peaceful South," although peace was achieved only when the descendants of the northern invaders, Oriental Annamese, submitted to their new masters, whoever they might be.

In a later century the French came to colonize. They governed the Annamese with strictness; not so the tribal villages. The colonial system required little of th. tribesmen, living as they did beyond mountain walls and moats of cavernous valleys, except the taxes which the French exacted in the form of building roads.

Each year a man gave a half cycle of the moon in such work. This was true of all the tribes in Indo-China. For some of them the French, in return, provided schools and medicine, but not for the tribes in Dalat's province.

"Why waste good piasters?" the colonials asked with a shrug.

The mountains were too steep and the people too remote for the government to send teachers or doctors to them. Besides, did these ignorant savages of the hills have minds worth worrying over? Or even souls? Better to leave such creatures to their preoccupations with evil spirits, their alcohol jars, and their bloody sacrificial feasts.

There was an exception, however: the ranks of the road builders must stay filled. The mind of the tribesman might be nothing in the opinion of the *commissionaires* and *commandants*, but his back was strong and his hand calloused. As clans emerged from mountain villages to trade wild berries and bulbs for salt or a castoff umbrella, or perhaps a water buffalo for a brass gong, the French recruited them for labor. It never occurred to the tribesman to refuse to work. Indeed, if he did not come out to trade, he often came out to work just because he knew it was expected of him.

Because the residents of Dalat knew the tribesman as tractable, they would now be caught unawares by this sudden rampage of mountain men led by the sorcerer. Usually a tribesman's violence was directed at a personal enemy. He might slip under another's house at night and settle an old score by thrusting a spear through the cracks in the bamboo floor and into his foe's kidney.

Unlike most of his tribespeople, Sau, on his trips to Dalat, often visited in the homes and offices of the Annamese and white men. The other tribesmen knew little of the ways of other people, nor did they care. World prosperity or calamity did not affect them at all. They lived an isolated life high up in the hills. Each family had a small patch of sloping ground on which to raise mountain rice and corn. But laying in a supply of food was hard. The soil was rocky, the weather harsh. And if a man laid by enough to purchase a couple of buffalo, the sorcerer's demand that he sacrifice them to ward off evil spirits made him poor again. When all his chickens and pigs and buffalo were gone and he still had not paid what he had promised, he borrowed.

Most of the tribesmen, therefore, were never free of debt. The sacrifices had kept Sau's father poor. This was largely because of Sau, for he had been born sickly. On the eighth day of his life, even before the naming ceremony, his father killed a buffalo. It was his hope that through the act of shedding blood and smearing it on the doorposts of his house and on the infant's forehead, his son would be spared.

At the ceremony the brother of Sau's mother chose to call the boy Ja Bang—"Barter." Following tradition, the uncle dipped the intestine of a fresh-killed chicken in rice alcohol and threw it at a rope suspended from the ceiling. His aim was good, the viscera twined around the rope; the name stuck.

The lad remained frail throughout his boyhood. His father performed sacrifice after bloody sacrifice by trading all he had for them and borrowing when it was gone.

Once Sau's father managed to gather enough mushrooms to make a trip to the market in Dalat worth while. Sau rode to town on his father's back. From the head of the long single file of villagers he saw for the first time a road that was wider and straighter than a trail through the hills. On this road that led into Dalat four columns such as theirs could walk abreast!

He sooned learned that this wonderful road led to even greater magnificence.

From his perch on his father's back Sau discovered there was much for a boy of six to behold. Past row upon row of tea bushes they walked, past neat gardens of rich green and yellow vegetables, past houses that sat in the middle of the gardens. What were these houses

like inside? Sau could only imagine how different from a village long-house they must be.

"What's that? . . . And that? . . . And that?" the boy asked in a near delirium of delight. Sau hardly knew where to look first—down the wide road divided by a long, narrow garden of bright blossoms down the middle; at the lakes, so much bigger and brighter than the mountain waters; or at the splendid houses.

He decided that he liked the houses best. One in particular was his favorite. His eye swept past its arched gateway, gay with lavender flowers, past its smooth expanse of grass and vista of road, to the house itself, the tallest and widest he had ever seen. Bright yellow, it stood out against the dark green of pine trees. A white-flowering frangipani grew at its door.

While his wondering eyes were taking in this grandeur, the door of the house suddenly opened. A man and a woman came out. They were unlike anybody young Sau had ever seen. Their skin was strangely pale. These were not the people of the mountains; nor were they the Annamese, who on one rare occasion he had seen in his village. They must be gods, he thought, they could only be gods. And this splendorous house was where they lived. God-people living in God-houses!

As Sau watched, two strange beings entered some mysterious object for which he had no name. The object made a slight moaning sound and moved away from the house and onto the road on which Sau's people walked. Some of the villagers jumped into a ditch as the thing sped past them. His father, however, only gave it wide berth. He called it *l'automobile;* having seen automobiles before, he was not afraid.

Something else caught Sau's eye that he had never seen before, a two-wheeled cart pulled by a diminutive horse.

The file of villagers moved on and Sau drank in more bewildering sights. Setting him down and taking him by the hand, his all-knowing father explained them as best he could. There were the barracks of the military; the office of the *résident-maire;* a building where the French residents worshiped the God of Heaven; the open-front shops with uncountable items that captivated the eye. The people looked strange, too.

"The ones with light skins," his father said to Sau, "are white people. You will see more of them here."

c

Sau's father led him straight past all this, past the noisy automobiles and on to the town market. Here was the broadest expanse of roof —made of iron, not of thatch—that the boy had ever seen. Under it he noticed the brown-yellow faces of the Annamese and the darker skins of tribesfolk from other mountain villages. Here and there among the stalls were groups of squatting tribesmen. The men gossiped amicably and puffed on their short-stemmed silver-inlaid pipes. The women in their hand-woven skirts of black, blue, and red cotton displayed meager wares of chickens and mushrooms and a pig or two on crude wooden stands or on mats on the ground. They, too, talked and smoked, and seemed more intent on nursing their babies than on trading.

Sau wandered through the market. He saw an Annamese man corner a tribesman and trade him two leaves of tobacco for a pig. There were many children. They wore garments like those of their elders, white or black skirts and trousers, cone-shaped hats of straw, and sandals. How odd for children to be clothed! He watched them play until he realized they had stopped and were looking at him and giggling.

He turned away from them; for the first time in his life he felt shame for his nakedness.

That night Sau's people walked to a place on the far side of the town where they were allowed to sleep on open ground. They wrapped themselves tightly in blankets the women had carried on their backs along with babies and trade goods. Everyone lay with feet toward the several campfires, like spokes of a wheel on a pony cart.

Sau spent two night in Dalat. The second night he saw that all the Annamese children in the street were busy with some secret project of their own. While he watched, they put on red paper costumes. Screaming and laughing, they became the feet of a long dragon that bobbed in and out among the lighted houses and shops. Then, carrying paper lanterns, they ran from house to house and danced until the householders brought treats of candied coconut and ginger-coated lotus seeds. How he wished he could join them!

Sleep hardly came for the boy that night, or for many nights afterward back home in his village. This world he had seen! Oh, to have clothes someday, a yellow-plastered house to live in, perhaps a pony cart to ride in up and down the wide, wide road!

In these years Sau's family lived in a village called Du Da Ti—Monkey Village, named after the lively creatures that played in the surrounding forest. The monkeys were friendly; it was the tigers everyone feared. The big bold creatures attacked the village pigs and goats and sometimes a child or even a man. They made life nearly unbearable. One never spoke the word "tiger" aloud; by doing so he could incite the spirit of the beast to fresh assault.

"Last night, out at the spring, did you hear—?" And the speaker would drop his voice and make the claws of a tiger with his fingers.

One evening Sau's father brought home a bird from the forest for his family's supper. While Sau's mother stirred up the fire, the bird lay on the bamboo floor, dripping blood through the slats to the ground beneath. That night, as everyone slept, a huge striped cat strode brazenly into the village. The scent of dried blood had beckoned the beast.

In terror the family awoke. Sau's father sprang to his knees.

"Who shook me?" he called out in the dark.

"They shook me, too," Sau's mother replied in a frightened whisper. By the glow of the firebox they both looked about; no unfamiliar shadow was there. Then through the flimsy floor they caught the cold blue flame of an eye. Stiffened with fright, they watched a shadow lunge at the underside of the floor where the bird had lain. Suddenly, they felt again the shaking that had aroused them; the tiger ripped at the floor with teeth and claws and the thin timbers beneath them trembled. Sau and his brother Kar shrieked.

"The house is falling!" Sau cried.

"Not yet it isn't," his father said, trying to reassure his family. But it seemed certain the floor would break and they would all fall through it—down within reach of the blood-hungry creature.

Sensing now that its midnight meal could be more than the drip from a bird, the tiger soon tore a hole in the floor and was swiping at it again and again. The hole grew dangerously larger. Sau and Kar huddled close in their mother's arms, their sobs mingling with the frenzied snorts of the beast below. What could two small boys do in the face of death but cry? What could anyone do?

Sau's father, knowing what to do, reached for his shoulder ax, a tool of many uses. Gripping it tightly, he crept toward the hole.

Sau knew he had to do more than cry. If his father fell victim to the beast, Sau himself would have to be his family's defender. Choking back the sobs, he stole a step from his mother and felt among the few utensils for a long-bladed knife. He might die in the attempt, but first he would fight the tiger.

At that moment Sau's father brought down one heavy, slashing blow that turned the contest in their favor. Yelping with pain, the wounded animal bounded off. The little family followed its anguished cries until they died away in the depths of the forest, and only in the restored silence of the night did they breathe more easily.

They had won out over their enemy. But enough was enough. In a day or two Sau's father moved his family from Monkey Village to a new home in a village of ten longhouses nestled in a bowl-like valley surrounded by sixteen mountain peaks.

Sau's mother and father carried the frail boy to the new home, which was a long day's walk from Monkey Village and two days by trail from Dalat. There the family enjoyed more abundant food and a better climate—though the sun never struck the village until the morning was half gone and the goats hugged a ridge to get the first rays as they came over the mountains.

Sau gradually grew stronger. By the time he was a youth he had more than made up for the delicacy of his boyhood. He became adept at every activity in the mountain countryside. With Kar he swam in the cold mountain streams, and often they vied to see who could stay under water longer. They boxed, hitting with the open hand. They made their own crossbows and with them shot squirrels in the corn and birds in the tall trees of the forest.

During all his growing up Sau never forgot the wonders that had once moved him in Dalat. He tried to explain the city's splendor to Kar, but his young brother seldom listened. Kar seemed more interested in perfecting a wooden spear to use on fish in the rock-filled streams. When Sau went from boyhood into youth, his name was changed from Barter to Sau, meaning grandchild. By doing so, his parents deprived the spirits of knowing that their son's sickness had ended.

More and more Sau helped the village men. Before long he was frequently taking the lead in doing communal chores. Near the end of every dry season the men cut down a sloping patch of forest to make it into a field for raising dry rice. After a moon's full cycle they started the fire which burned until it had eaten away the felled trees.

Then came a serious game in which all in the village listened for the season's final song of the Precious Bird. Few ever saw this gray-black creature with streak of white; mostly it stayed in the very tops of the tallest trees. But all heard its four-tone whistle—until one day someone noted that the bird had not sung. After seven days of silence it was time to drop the seed rice into holes in the burned-over ground —and then let the timely rains do the rest.

Sau worked hard at field chores, but his mind was not on his labors. As he watched the great flames lick at the trees, he pretended that these flicks of flame were lamps, lighting the windows of the great villas in Dalat. In his mind he did not walk the field to poke holes in the ground for his rice grains; he took, instead, giant steps on the broad road that led into town. The three or four water buffalo that he herded for other villagers became the tiny horses that carted Annamese families through the busy streets.

Sau was fifteen when his mother died. Under the tribal rule of maternal succession he was no longer his father's child. Had he been younger he would have become the son of a relative of his mother.

But he was quite grown up now; he wore a loincloth and had cropped close his curly hair. At his age, he was on his own. He could go where he wished, do what he wanted. With this freedom before him, he asked himself what had been the most wonderful thing that ever happened to him. It was, of course, his boyhood trip to Dalat. Why not go there again? He decided he would. But he must have a reason for going.

A blustery wind was blowing across the mountain peaks. Sau suffered from the cold. He found this reason enough, when he had harvested his rice, to take his crop to market in Dalat to trade for a blanket.

This time the houses did not appear so tall, nor the road so wide. Still, the richness of Dalat—rich by comparison with the villages he had known—held for him a sweet fascination. He thought he might like to stay. But he would have to devise a means to do so. He could say he wanted to go to school—but where did a tribesman go to school?

Whatever his excuse, he made up his mind. And in staying, he was to discover that Dalat was more than pretty houses with flowering frangipani, more than articles to be seen and handled in the shops.

He was to find here a new direction for his life.

In a day or two he completed his trading. Still the market was like a magnet, drawing him for days afterward from the field where the tribesmen camped. One morning Sau loitered there. A small man on a bicycle spotted him. With an air of decision the man leaped off his wheel and walked it straight to where Sau stood. Although the man was fully clothed in the loose white trousers and tunic of the Annamese, he was of brown skin. His receding hair made his full, round face seem rounder. He had deep-set lines along his nose and mouth. He smiled broadly. To Sau, he seemed friendly. But Sau had not forgotten how he once saw an Annamese slyly get a pig for a little tobacco, and now he wondered whether this tribesman who had taken on the garb of the Annamese might not behave like one.

He warned himself to be on guard.

"You, there," the small man said in a dialect resembling Sau's. His smiling manner had changed to gruffness. He poked Sau in the chest with a stubby finger. "Do you know how to wash clothes?"

"Yes, I know how to wash clothes," replied the youth. He tried to sound as harsh and abrupt as his questioner.

"Can you drive an ox? Can you fell trees? Can you sit still long enough to learn to read?"

The little man shot his questions rapidly and Sau, thinking quick replies were needed to defend himself, replied with a hurried "yes" to each query.

"Come with me," the man ordered. "You'll be fed, and you'll be given a place to sleep. I myself will teach you out of a book."

Sau was trapped. His answers had placed him in the stranger's power. He was angry at himself.

But what was it the man had said about learning? None of his people had any learning. Sau had always wanted to have an ear for words. There were no books in his tongue to learn from. But this man had said he would teach Sau. To work for him would make it possible for Sau to remain here in Dalat—and to learn too! It all seemed like a dream.

Sau had no idea who the man was; but in that moment he suddenly felt a kinship to him.

Picking up the basket that contained his blanket and his few belongings, he followed the brusk little man. Sau thought him considerate to walk his wheel alongside him, even though he said nothing more. Sau had no idea where they were going but he kept on, past the paved boulevard with its flower gardens and onto a dirt road. This road brought them to a tawny, tall house standing in the midst of several outbuildings.

They did not go to the main house, but to a low, thatch-roofed rambling shack of rough boards. The small man told Sau to put down his basket, and then handed him a pair of old trousers. Sau took off his loincloth—as if he were never to wear it again—put on the trousers, and was ready for work.

His first job was to gather wood, then to make a fire under a giant caldron of water. From the house the little man brought armloads of clothing; he showed Sau how to soap and boil the garments, then to rinse and hang them on bushes to dry.

Sau learned the man's name was K'Sol, and that though he was not of Sau's tribe their language and customs were similar. From other tribesmen working around the property he learned that K'Sol was foreman for a white foreigner named Jackson. Ong Jackson—Mr. Jackson—was a kind man to work for, the men said. But look out for K'Sol if Ong wasn't around!

Sau's next job was to drive a two-wheeled oxcart to the main boulevard and there to tap a cock to fill the water barrel balanced on the cart. By making several trips he replenished the laundry water and brought up the level of a cistern serving the main house.

Once, while driving his cart to the cistern, he had his first glimpse of Jackson. He saw him through an open window of a corner room in the house. How pale the man's face was, and how thin his hair! Sau had to stop the cart and sit and stare at him.

Jackson sat alone at a big table; yet Sau heard him talking as though someone were in the room with him. Then Sau noticed he was talking to the end of a black stick held to his mouth and ear.

Sau could not understand the words, but they were pouring forth fast and loud as Jackson waved his arm in wide gestures while he spoke. Then suddenly this odd man took the stick from his face and laid it in a kind of cradle. He looked up to see Sau staring at him. He grinned, and the smile spread over his whole face. Sau grinned back and moved on.

When the sun had climbed nearly to its zenith, Jackson strode out of the house. He spoke briefly to K'Sol, who then called Sau and two other workers to come and sit with him on a newly terraced bank of earth. Jackson spoke in Annamese, which K'Sol knew and could translate into Sau's tribal tongue. Through K'Sol, Jackson told them of the earth and sky and how they had been created. At the end he confided that he knew the One who had made these marvels.

What a strange way for a man to talk, thought Sau. So far he understood very little. But it made him curious. He wanted to know more.

For many days Sau washed clothes and hauled water. Then he was given other jobs. He terraced the hillside down from the house, cut back jungle in the ravine below the property, helped erect buildings. He was eager to learn, and to practice what he had learned. Early every morning Jackson came out of his house to where the men worked and showed them how to use the hammer and saw. When the sun stood high overhead and again when it dipped behind the mountains, he called them together to tell more about this mysterious One who made not only heaven and earth, but the tribesmen themselves.

Sau was amazed. Didn't this man—whom he now called Grandfather—know that the first tribesmen had crawled from holes in the ground? Sau's father had explained to him once that their ancestors were so slow in climbing out that when they got here all the good land of the earth had already been taken by others. Only the mountains were left to the tribes.

Sau learned that his teacher's full name was Herbert A. Jackson, and that his wife was named Lydia. They were members of the Christian and Missionary Alliance; like many of that group in America, they had crossed an ocean to tell people that the creator was the God of Heaven and that God loved the people He made.

The Jacksons had first settled in this land far to the south in the hot, wet delta of the Mekong River. Once they went north to visit and, on the return trip, stopped to rest in Dalat. There, on the road to the market, Jackson saw a sight that intrigued him. Before him trooped a single line of brawny, bronzed men in loincloths, followed by their goats, pigs, and chickens, and by their black-skirted women and naked children.

He was impressed by the bearing and rugged appearance of the men. In the faces of both the men and women he thought he noticed a straightforward look. Yet their eyes seemed brimming with sadness.

Stopping a French official who happened by at the moment, Jackson asked excitedly:

"M'sieur, who are these people?"

"Who are they?" the Frenchman replied with some annoyance. *"Zut!* They're really nobody. We pay scant attention to tribesmen here."

So these were the tribesmen of Indo-China—the mysterious, almost unknown people of the mountains! They fascinated Jackson. He felt himself deeply stirred inside, rebelling against the officer's remark. So fine-looking a people and they were called nobody!

He watched until they faded from view. Then he all but ran to the hotel to tell his wife that he wanted her to go with him to the market.

"Lydia, dear," he said as they hurried along, "you've heard of the mountain tribesmen. Well, I've just seen some for the first time in my life!"

Jackson could not get these people out of his mind. The missionary couple went back later to their work in the flatlands of the south, but they often talked of the tribespeople of Dalat.

"Do you know, Lydia," Jackson said one day, "I've learned some more about those mountainfolk. I hear that they live in daily terror of evil spirits. It seems to me that they need, above all, to be told about Christ."

But it was a long time before he could free himself from a busy schedule of missionary activity among the Annamese. For eight years he kept urging the mission to begin a ministry among the tribespeople. But there was no one whom the mission could spare from other work.

Then one day the Jacksons' son became ill. The doctor prescribed the cooler climate of Dalat, which, though lower than the mountain peaks around it, stood more than a kilometer above sea level. For their son's sake they had to leave their work in the south. Arriving in Dalat, Jackson again promptly brought up to the mission leaders the subject of the tribesmen.

"We're here in the middle of these abandoned people," he said. "Can't we start a Gospel witness among them?"

Permission was granted—from the mission, not from the government. Soon Jackson was trying everything he knew to make friendly contact. Once a woman asked him to buy a wild orchid, a flower the tribesmen took for granted but which they discovered foreigners were fond of. Jackson gladly bought it. Then he was deluged with orchids. By the end of the day he owned fourteen plants.

Another time he bought the shell corn a man offered. It was a contact, although he had no use for the corn. None, that is, until the following day. That afternoon he bought a horse from still another tribesman, and fed the corn to the animal.

Word passed throughout the market that there was a white man in Dalat who did not kick or beat a tribesman. In fact, he paid the tribesmen real piasters for working, and for sitting and listening while he talked. Soon after that, when the day's bartering was over, half a village at a time was camping on Jackson's land.

In this way "the tribes center" began.

Jackson was kind to the mountainfolk because he loved them. And he felt there was no greater demand on his love than their need to hear that God was good and could master all their evil spirits. To tell them about God, this good Spirit of the Skies, he needed to translate the Bible, the book that revealed God, into their language. But their language had never been set down on paper. The spirits had once scratched the markings of the tribesman's tongue on a buffalo hide, the people said. The careless man in charge of the precious hide left it outside one night and the hungry village dogs devoured it.

For some time Jackson had prayed, "Lord, send me a tribesman who can speak Annamese, the tongue of this land that I know. I want the best man possible to do this job."

K'Sol was the man—a small man, but when Jackson first got hold of him a tiger in loincloth!

He was ruthless, shrewd, a lover of the alcohol jar, profane, proud, possessor of a fiery temper. He loaned his money to other tribesmen —his money for their children, who became his slaves. But he knew men—he had been boss of a road gang. And he had an ear for languages—Annamese, French, and several tribal dialects besides his own.

Soon, Jackson and a half-tamed K'Sol were spending hours each day at a table by themselves. They jabbered at each other; often it seemed they would end in blows. One day Sau saw Grandfather stand up and peer into K'Sol's mouth and throat. He explained to K'Sol that he was looking to see how he made the sounds peculiar to the tribal language.

In a rage K'Sol jumped up from the table.

"Give me a hammer! Give me a shovel!" he shouted. "Work with these tools I can do, but to sit and let someone look into my throat I will not!"

Nevertheless, he was pleased that someone took an interest in his language. So the next day he resumed. He continued to help Jackson put the Bible into the tribal tongue. One day Sau noted a change in K'Sol. When he passed on Grandfather's words about God, he spoke as if he was acquainted with Him.

Later Sau questioned him. He learned that K'Sol had indeed changed. This fierce little man had become a believer in the God of Heaven; as the tribesmen said in speaking of a convert—a God-Follower.

Not long after this Sau declared that he, too, believed. He said it because Jackson had been good to him and Sau knew that the missionary wanted him to believe. And Sau said he believed partly because K'Sol had told him to believe, just as at other times K'Sol told him to cut down a tree or to dig steps in the side of a hill. K'Sol had changed in most of his ways, but this one-time tiger was not yet a bleating kid; he could still grow angry quickly and throw a rock at one who roused him, or go after the person with a stick.

With Grandfather, Sau was ashamed not to believe; with K'Sol, whom he alternately feared and idolized, he was both ashamed and afraid not to believe.

In this state of having been taught, but not yet understanding, Sau went home on a visit to Sixteen Peaks. To his sorrow, he found many of his kin dreadfully sick. Some had sacrificed nearly all the buffalo they possessed, but even the caked, dried blood on foreheads and arms did not drive out the fevers and aches.

Sau entered the house of a sufferer and stood by the mat on which he lay writhing in pain.

"Uncle," he said respectfully to the man who was older than he, "you need to pray to the God of Heaven." The man was too sick to pay him much attention.

He approached a granny. Eager to show her the respect due her age, he said to her, "Doubly old mother, I wish to talk about you to the Spirit of the Skies." She ignored him.

Everywhere he went whether they paid him any heed or not, he prayed for the sick. Evidently his prayers were answered; within days even the most languid was up and about.

One day Kar approached him, almost with trepidation.

"Older brother," said this youth who was ordinarily so playful and jolly, but who was now seriously seeking an explanation of Sau's seemingly strange powers. "When the sacrifices could not bring health to the sick, why did your calling on the God of Heaven make them well?"

Sau looked vacantly at his brother, unable to reply.

"Does a powerful demon live in your body?" In asking, Kar spoke as if he hoped this was not true. The folk who gave evidence of housing a particular spirit or of possessing the miraculous power to become a tiger when they tired of being a mere man—these folk were killed by their fellow villagers or driven to a life of wandering alone in the forests. Kar hoped his own brother wasn't one of these— but how could he be sure?

Sau could say only that he did not know why the people had got well when he prayed. Sau, as greatly perplexed as his brother, returned to his work in Dalat. He made up his mind to learn—*really* learn—about this strange and wonderful One named Jesus and about *His* sacrifice.

At rest periods, as Jackson taught the tribesmen, he listened intently. In the evening, after the work was done, he paid attention to K'Sol who, with new patience and tenderness, repeated to them the Bible lessons that Lydia Jackson had taught him during the day.

K'Sol, by using in his speech the particulars of nature that each of them knew so well, was able to make things clear to them.

"Our people kill because they mean to kill," K'Sol said. "A man kills a deer for its hide. He kills another man because he hates him." K'Sol knew the tribesmen well. And why not? Was there anything in his lifetime he had not done?

"Men leave their wives for other men's wives," he continued.

"They do," acknowledged one of his pupils, "but for his adultery a man pays his wife's family dearly."

"Thirteen buffalo—that is what an uncle of mine paid his old mother-in-law," added another.

They pay, Sau said to himself, and they go right on doing wrong. Was it wrong to leave one's wife for another? Did not all the men do it? But if it was not wrong, why did they pay? Sau made up his mind that it *was* wrong—yet men did not seem to be sorry for their wrong.

K'Sol looked at the young tribesmen before him; he so earnestly wanted them to understand. "You turn your eyes-nose away from God," he said, explaining in their doublets that they tried to hide their faces from a searching God. "You need to stop turning away. Only God can make you want to do right."

Sometimes the young men sat alone around their outdoor fires at night or in the crude house of slab boards and thatch—"the tribes center," all were now calling it. At other times the regulars were joined by whole clans in for a visit from the hills. Whether few or many, they talked over the things that Grandfather and K'Sol had taught them.

"If God made the frog," reasoned Sau one night, "it should be God we worship, not the frog."

A second youth was more cautious.

"The Spirit of the Skies is good and will not harm us," he said. "God once lifted the heavens off the earth, and our ancestors worshiped Him then. But as time went on they worshiped Him less and less. They chose, instead, to worship the things that this greatest of spirits made."

"Yes," another joined in, "it is the spirits of those creatures that can harm us. It is to them that I intend to offer *my* sacrifice." The fear of vindictive spirits and abandonment to inevitable fate prevented him from trusting wholly in Heaven's God.

While each of the men felt K'Sol's influence, Sau felt it even more. From K'Sol, Sau learned to work hard and to enjoy working. Others might saunter around the tribes center; Sau ran more than he walked. Always he was first on the job. In washing clothes he learned neatness; in polishing shoes and pressing trousers he acquired personal tidiness, even though it was not always his lot to wear fine clothes. K'Sol taught Sau to be honorable and virtuous. He was strict about Sau's associates, and insisted that the young man return from the market within the time allowed for a buying trip. Many times Sau ran all the way to reach home in time.

Now it wasn't so much that Sau was afraid of K'Sol; it was because he loved the little man and did not want to disappoint him.

K'Sol made frequent trips to the villages of his people. Sau often went with him to carry his basket. On these trips he began to learn how to teach and preach.

"K'Sol is an Apostle Paul," Jackson remarked to his wife as he saw the two set out one day. "And Sau is his Timothy."

Whether at the tribes center, in which a school with scheduled classes had started, or in a pagan village they were visiting, K'Sol urged young Sau to study, to be faithful in his work, never to be satisfied with less than the best in anything he undertook.

One night Sau sat along by the fire in front of the old house at the center. He pondered a thought from the Bible that K'Sol had helped put into their tongue and that this believing tribesman then taught his pupil:

"Greater is he that is in you, than he that is in the world."

Sau repeated it over and over and thought about it far into the night. Just what did it mean?

The fire grew dim. Sau tossed a pitchy stick into the dying flame; at once it blazed with new life. With the sudden burst of light came understanding. He clapped his hands to his knees. In excitement he cracked each of his knuckles. Now he knew its meaning!

This great One, wasn't He in K'Sol? Hadn't He worked mighty changes in the little man that made Sau, for one, love and respect him instead of fear him? Hadn't God taken the selfish, scheming heart out of K'Sol, and his terrible temper, too, and in their place put compassionate understanding?

By K'Sol's own teaching—and Grandfather's—he knew that K'Sol wasn't the same man. It was as though the old K'Sol had died and in his place there now lived a new K'Sol.

As Sau thought of the new K'Sol, he began to find his own ear developing a taste for the delicious things it had heard of God. He was beginning to understand that not the evening song of the frog nor the sacrifice of a buffalo, but the spilled blood of the Son of Heaven's God, had given birth to the new K'Sol and now nurtured him, and this was what could give new life to Sau himself.

"I thank God that God loved me so much that God's Son died for me," he prayed, being careful not to dishonor God by using the pronouns of familiar speech.

Once he knew firmly that the blood of Christ washed away the sin of one's old self and in the wake of the cleansing the resurrected Christ came to live in the heart, once he had developed a "delicious ear" toward the Spirit of the Skies, he could hardly wait to walk the trail again to Sixteen Peaks. He went back home once more.

This time he told the people eagerly what he had not been able to tell them before—that Jesus healed bodies, yes, but more important, that Jesus Christ could be a greater force in their lives than the most powerful of the spirits that held them captive since birth.

But it was their choice to make, just as it had been his, to accept or reject the new life in Christ that God held out to them.

Sau's people began to see a smile come to the young man's face. After a while they noticed that the smile seldom left, and when it did it soon returned. On one of Sau's visits to his home, he tried to explain his faith to Kar, but somehow Kar did not seem to understand. This made the smile disappear from Sau's face for a time. But when Kar asked that he keep on teaching him, Sau smiled again.

"Older brother, I do not have it yet," Kar said earnestly and not with despair, "but someday I will. Then I will go with you to Dalat where you got your delicious ear."

That promise had been given five years before, and Kar had not yet walked the trail to the tribes center, now a scattering of small, plain buildings—until today.

Sau motioned for Kar to stop. The rough and rocky trail was behind them; the way ahead was now smooth.

"Rest," he said. "We are coming to the junction. You stay here while I see if the marching band has arrived—or if the men have already passed by here."

Cautiously, he crept through the tangled underbrush. In a minute now, he would know who was winning the fateful race to Dalat. There was reason to hope that the drunken villagers, like themselves, might have been slowed by the rain and the hail. Yet, he knew that since the other route was the more traveled one, it would be packed harder and it would not so quickly turn to mire.

He pushed aside a large fern. Before him stretched the path from the sorcerer's village. Up and down the trail as far as he could see were the muddy prints of naked feet.

The sorcerer's men had already passed this point and were ahead in the dash to Dalat!

The brothers had hardly paused since their start. Sau's body craved surcease as much as Kar's. He went back to his brother and for a moment sat on a rock next to where Kar drowsed. As he rested the thought came to him: What right had they to think of their tired bodies when the very lives of others depended on them?

Sau was on his feet. He tugged at Kar's shoulder.

"We'll rest another time. Let's go before we are too late."

Kar found himself still groggy and reluctant, but obeying. He, too, was on his feet. He went to pick up the bamboo basket. Sau kicked it aside.

"Never mind it," he said. "We'll have no time to camp tonight."

The basket contained food; they could get on without that. Plenty of time tomorrow, after they had given their warning . . . In the pack, too, were gifts for Grandmother and Grandfather, the yams and the tasty green bananas. Other gifts could be brought another time. *Another time.* There would be no other time if they failed. The crazed mountain men would kill the Jacksons—and the *résident-maire* and the lesser Frenchmen of the colonial government and the women and children of the city, anyone their frenzy told them to kill.

Now he was appalled by a thought which had not occurred to him before.

Without doubt, he said to himself, the tribesmen could kill many at first, because they would be taking the city by surprise. But the surprise would not last long. Those who ruled the country had by far the superior forces. Retaliation would be swift and deadly. Sau knew that just outside Dalat the French soldiers kept several air-planes. He knew, too, that as the planes flew, fire and destruction were sometimes dropped from their bellies onto targets below.

For every person the tribesmen killed, a whole mountain village would become a target.

When the mountainfolk heard the planes coming, they in their desperation could do no more than throw their pointed sticks into the air or futilely shoot their arrows at the swift, high-flying birds.

His mission was not just to warn his friends of threatening death, and through them to warn others; it was to save his own people, too, those who weren't ready to die, even those whose captive wills had brought this nightmare upon them all.

Sau half turned to his brother and whistled sharply. He sprang over a fallen tree and broke into a run. Kar followed close on his heels.

3

Someday . . . Only God

Dawn flooded the sky in the east as the weary brothers left the muddy trail for the road of crushed stone. No more plodding through the tangled brush and slogging through swamps on their short-cut path; no more battling mosquitoes and giant jungle flies; no more stopping to cut away the bloodsuckers that clamped onto their legs and arms and even necks and middles.

The two should have drawn comfort from the prospect of open country and hard road underfoot. Yet, they could not breathe freely until they knew that Dalat had awakened to a pleasant day and not to the horror of savage assault.

In the first rays of sunlight they approached the military *poste,* a whitewashed, mud-plastered tower, looming like a square lighthouse some twenty feet high, with an open port on each side. A tricolor flew from its shabbily thatched roof. This was the farthest French outreach, about an hour from Dalat. Here they ought to learn whether they had been able to forge ahead in the race against the insurrectionists.

Annamese guards manned hundreds of such checkpoints throughout the country. Usually the queues of mountain people on their way into town passed under the scrutiny of the sentries.

But today there was no sign of life anywhere. It occurred to Sau that marching men might have taken it by storm, slain the sentries, and passed on.

Kar and he quickened pace. They did not run; if someone was in there they did not want to arouse suspicion. So, walking fast but discreetly, they soon drew even with the tower, circled to the door that led to the inside ladder, and nearly tripped over two soldiers who in ill-fitting uniforms sat on the ground and leaned against the dew-damp walls.

The rifle of one lay across his lap; he slept. The other, unarmed, sat chewing betel nut. No doubt the pair stayed awake by turns to listen for the lorry that at some time during the morning would bring the French sergeant and the guard relief. Sau grinned and swept past as if making for a drink at a nearby pool. To this intrusion the awake but lethargic sentry responded by drawing his knees up under his chin and giving the brothers an indolent stare. One look at him and Sau knew that all so far was well.

They dared not stop to explain their mission. They had to push on. As Sau thought about it, perhaps the sorcerer and his crew would not come this way at all. Perhaps they had chosen to circle wide around the *poste* and follow one of the several deep valleys that led into Dalat.

Who was to say they had not dispersed, traveling by various routes, and were even now entering the town?

The brothers moved quickly along the main road and into Dalat. The final stretch, the unpaved road leading to the tribes center, they covered in a run.

Going straight to the headquarters building, they broke in on a scene already charged with high tension. Other men had come in from the mountains with similar stories of python worship.

" 'Eat only one kernel of corn a day.' This is what the mysterious traveler instructed the sorcerer of our village to tell us," said one named Krong. "Already some of our people are sick from hunger."

"The people obey. They are in the sorcerer's power," said another called Tieng.

Sau knew these men well. Krong came from a village two days' walk from Sixteen Peaks; Tieng from one nearer by. He knew them to be men careful with the truth. He did not doubt what they said. Did it not agree with what he himself knew?

Quickly Sau sized up the situation.

The mountain seethed. Once Sau had seen a can of gasoline explode and hurl its fire over a wide expanse. The cult of the python was spreading like fire; only fast action would halt its deadly progress. If only K'Sol had not gone to visit his people! But he was away— Sau would have to take the lead.

He chose Krong, Krong's brother Chu, and a third young man named Kring to go with him to tell the missionary. Each of these

SOMEDAY . . . ONLY GOD

had seen the worship of the snake and could testify that trouble
blazed in the hills. Tired as he was from the trip, Sau hustled the men
out of the headquarters and led the way to the main house.

He knew where to find Grandfather. He went directly to the
window of the corner room. Grandfather was there, all right, studying
at his desk. Seeing the men approach, Jackson laid down his books
and came to the window.

"What's the matter?" he demanded. In this land it was customary
to spend much time in exchanging greetings before coming around to
business. But Jackson wasn't a man to stand on ceremony.

Sau did the explaining. When he came to the part about the armed
men closing on the city, Jackson broke in:

"Are you sure?"

Not waiting for an answer, Jackson crossed to his desk, picked up
the handpiece of a French telephone—the "stick" that once had
puzzled Sau—and fairly exploded into it:

"*Numero un, s'il vous plait . . . immediatement!*"

After a delay not unreasonable for a colonial telephone system he
was connected to the *résident-maire*.

"*Allo, allo.* Pastor Jackson here. *M'sieur,* it is to your vital interest
that you allow me an appointment—immediately," he said in French,
barking most undiplomatically. "And you must permit me to bring
four tribesmen."

Presently he slammed down the telephone and headed for the door.

"Get in the car," he said to the men.

They had ridden in the missionary's ancient Ford before, but never
had known it would go so fast. Over the dusty mission road they
bumped, onto the flower-lined boulevard. The office of the *résident-
maire* was situated in a low, rambling building near the post office
and across from the French church. In one flowing motion Jackson
ground the car to a stop, cut the engine, and bounded toward the
building entrance, all before a wide-eyed Annamese doorkeeper.

"Tell *m'sieur* that Pastor Jackson is here to see him," the missionary said in the man's own language. Jackson's relations with colonial
officialdom were cordial and gave him access, though the attention
he paid the *mois*—"those savages"—annoyed the government.

The *résident-maire* had once complained:

"*Pasteur,* those wild men are hard enough to rule without your

filling their heads with ideas. And must you encourage them to come
into town? My flower beds—*Sacré Bleu!* It's easier to control the
instincts of their dogs . . ."

But missionary and tribesmen were now ushered past numerous
male secretaries filling the large central room—French civil servants
who breathed polite oaths that such a delegation should pass before
them and on into the private chamber of the city's ranking official.
In his office Bonnet, the mayor, rose from behind mounds of papers
spread over his huge oak desk, motioned for Jackson to be seated,
ignored the tribesmen, restacked the papers to give him a line of
sight, and sat down again. He wrinkled his nose, swiping a hand over
his sparse, graying hair.

"*M'sieur le pasteur*—"

He spoke politely but with coolness. He wanted to convey his
disapproval at dragging those ragtag tribesmen into the serenity of his
office. He clearly would have preferred to receive the American at
a more civilized hour and in a more sociable setting.

But Jackson was not inclined this morning to observe protocol.

"*M'sieur,*" said Jackson with directness—he used only a fraction
of his chair to sit on—"these men have come to report strange and
mysterious happenings in the mountains."

"Such as what?" the Frenchman inquired without interest, trying
to conceal his annoyance beneath official courtesy.

"Sau here," Jackson went on, "brings word that at this very
moment a large band of mountain men is marching on Dalat. They
may number hundreds by now. They are armed. They are drunk.
They are dangerous."

"But why?" the mayor asked in bewilderment. "What is their
purpose?"

"They have been instructed by the sorcerer to kill everything
white," Jackson said with agitation. "They're coming to kill you
and every white person and Annamese."

Bonnet sprang to his feet, and in the process sent a stack of papers
cascading to the floor.

"*Incroyable!*" he cried.

"Ask *him!*" challenged Jackson, indicating Sau with a nod of his
head.

"*M'sieur le pasteur,* you know they are prone to exaggeration," the mayor countered, calming down and feeling quite justified in bringing the gullible American around to objectivity.

"Ask him!" Jackson, reddening, shot back again. "Ask him yourself! You've got your own interpreter."

"I will," replied the mayor. Turning to a hovering secretary, he directed that his tribal interpreter be brought in.

Sau, unable to hold back, started to add his voice to the heated exchange. Speaking with animation, part in his own tongue, part in a rudimentary French, he volunteered information on the march.

"Stop!" the mayor ordered. He no longer disbelieved; now he was afraid of missing facts that Sau was spouting bilingually.

Through his interpreter Bonnet fired a few questions at Sau, then curtly cut him off, telling him that that was enough for the present.

"Get me *le capitaine* on the telephone!" he snapped to his secretary.

A moment later the secretary handed him the phone.

"*Allo. M'sieur le capitaine?* I have just received grave news. A band of armed mountain men is marching on Dalat. I think you will want to alert your guards at once."

Having taken the needed action, he turned back to his visitors, the picture of the efficient colonial servant in full control of the situation. After all, this was not the first crisis of his assignment—though admittedly to deliver one's province from a savage uprising was not an everyday occurrence. He questioned the four tribesmen in turn about this strange phenomenon of python worship.

Sau told how the sorcerer had played upon the villagers' fear of evil spirits to gain their obedience to his will.

"An insurrection," the mayor said, arching his graying brows knowingly at Jackson. "An insurrection in the guise of religion." He turned to Sau.

"Do *you* worship the snake?" he demanded.

"No," replied Sau. "I trust in the God of Heaven."

Standing with the white men, Sau did not loom impressively tall, and his clothes were muddied from the trail (he had dipped his hands in a barrel of water at the tribes center to wash before coming in). To Jackson at that moment, however, Sau was the biggest man in the room. The mayor, too, was impressed by the forthrightness of his answer.

"You are quite right to believe in God," he said. He was thoroughly relaxed now. He had forgiven the intrusion, and a hint of gentleness crept into the tone of his voice.

"He teaches his people about God," Jackson put in.

"And do they learn?" Bonnet asked, hardly willing to go that far —to believe they did.

Sau told him that some in his village had given their hearts to Christ.

Christians? In a village of ignorant mountain men? Surely not . . . but these men standing in the mayor's office . . . these who came to him as they did . . . their action required a daring that he could hardly explain.

"Incroyable!"

This time he spoke softly and with more admiration than doubt. His manner became amiable. He smiled.

"I like it. I like it that you're honest Christians."

Then drawing himself up, resuming the full dignity of his office, he addressed a command to Sau:

"You, my man, go back to all your villages and teach your people more. Tell them that to worship the snake is bad for them. It will only bring them death."

To Jackson he said:

"I had thought that your teaching religion to these savages would upset their way of life and make them harder to govern. But today, I am not so sure."

He spoke once more to Sau:

"Tell your people it is the God of Heaven they should believe in."

Before they left, Jackson obtained a paper for the tribesmen stating that the bearers were Christians and that they should be neither harmed nor detained. It would get them by the aroused military, who now would be suspicious of every brown-skinned man. And with the raised insignia of the Indo-China government embossed in one corner, it might even impress hostile tribesmen.

Sau now had his white shirt and an official document tucked in its pocket as credentials. His shirt had been of no value at the python ritual two days before. His paper was still of uncertain worth.

"Will Grandfather pray for us?" Sau asked as they left the mayor's office. Grandfather had a way with God, he knew, and what clothes and paper might not accomplish God's power could.

"Grandfather will please take us to the end of the road," Sau said quietly, but earnestly, when they were all seated in Jackson's Ford. The missionary looked at Sau and thought he knew why his prayers were needed.

All that Sau observed on their way to the road's end assured him that Dalat and its people were now safe. Soldiers moved briskly into defensive positions. The town was alert. Lorries lumbered up and down the road, depositing both riflemen and ammunition boxes in strategic spots.

But now Sau had another concern on his mind—the fate of his own tribesmen. There was no question that they would be the ones to be killed if the marching column was ambushed by the angered soldiers.

At the end of the road Sau and his companions got out of the car. They paused to pray with the missionary. Then they said good-by to him and continued on the trail on foot.

Sau turned for a last wave to his friend. Grandfather sat uneasily at the wheel; Sau knew he would stop them from going, if he could. But he couldn't.

"Be careful—and God help you!" the missionary called after them. With this blessing in their ears, the four moved on. Sau walked in the lead in the direction of the warring column—it was somewhere up ahead.

The sun stood straight above when, from a well-chosen spot of concealment, Sau and his friends saw a sight that chilled his blood. The mad, chanting band of killers was marching forward in a single line, the sorcerer at their head. Sau crouched beside a boulder to watch them skirt a bamboo thicket, cross a small creek, and begin mounting the hill on which he and the others hid.

He gave a low whistle; he could see half a hundred men! And how many more were yet to come?

From their mud-caked legs he saw why they had taken so long to get here. But now they came steadily nearer. He felt the paper in his shirt pocket. He could step from the shelter of the rock and wave it, hoping by the shock of this maneuver to stop their march. He could squat low, and remain silent; the men would march right past him and the others and never know they were there. He could let them go to the end of the trail, to the road. They might get as far as the reinforced *poste,* but no farther.

At the head of the column, wearing his turban but not his cloth, the sorcerer led his men nearly abreast of Sau's rock. Sau's decision could not be delayed. The sorcerer raised his voice in a raucous chant:

"Oh, spirit of the worshipful python—"

"Oh, spirit of the worshipful python," intoned the forward men. Back down the line the chant passed.

"Accept the blood of your enemies," he sang.

Back down the hill the couplet ran, across the creek and around the clump of bamboo.

Sau took out the paper, unfolded it, and absently ran his finger across the raised insignia. Without looking about to see what his friends might do, he leaped from his place beside the rock into the sorcerer's path.

"Stop!" he commanded, waving the paper in the leader's face.

The sorcerer sprang back, nearly falling, petrified as if Sau had been a tiger. The men in the lead faltered. Those coming up behind them still chanted to the serpent; they had not heard Sau's command. Out of the corner of his eye, Sau saw the three white shirts of his friends at his elbow. It was good to know he was not alone.

He kept on waving the paper in front of the sorcerer. The old fellow knew nothing of what it said; he had recovered enough, though, to recognize the man who held it. Before he could curse him, Sau cried out:

"The *résident-maire* knows about you!" he shouted. "The military knows. You think you will attack! You will *be* attacked. You think you will surprise them? They will surprise *you*. The soldiers are armed and ready for you. Turn back or you will all be killed!"

As he spoke he realized that a single word from the sorcerer would unleash the fury of the mob that surrounded him and his companions. Once aroused, these men would pull his limbs from their sockets. Some reached out and grasped his arm. One word—that was all it would take.

"He's told them!" the sorcerer said. The quaver in his voice betrayed a fear greater than the lust for vengeance that had been in his chant.

"Maybe he's brought the soldiers with him," one screamed above the mob's cry.

"Their guns! Watch out for their guns!" shouted another.

The drink with which the men gorged themselves in the villages had long since worn off. What excited them now was a common intent to murder. But suddenly the spirit of the mob collapsed. Sau's unexpected appearance, his warning, and the confusion broke the spell of unity.

Each man now looked with fear at the rocks and trees lining the path, as though expecting these familiar objects to spew forth deadly fire. Sau was no longer important to them; neither was the mission on which they had entered so boldly. A few on the fringe had already fled. The flight grew into a rout until only the barest handful remained.

Among them were the sorcerer himself and three of his most ardent followers. Sensing that the white-shirted preachers were alone since no soldiers had sprung to their defense, he thought to dispose of them and move on. He muttered that he ought to run his knife through meddlesome Sau. But he did not. Lacking his armed following, he was afraid to try.

Never mind; frustrated though he was at the moment, he had other means of revenge than the knife and the shoulder ax. Who, after all, could withstand his magic?

Swinging on a bare and calloused heel, he rained oaths on the French, on the yellow men of Dalat, on Sau, on his God of Heaven.

"Someday your God may be your only protector," he said with contempt. Sau knew that it was not paper nor shirt, but the God of Heaven, who had protected him today.

Breathing thankfully that at last the day's work was done, Sau watched the sorcerer march off in the direction from which he had come. Those who had stood with the sorcerer turned, too. As they brushed past to go home, defeated, they showed faces to Sau that were the faces of vengeful men. He knew full well what menace they intended.

Yet, somehow, it didn't seem to matter. He was not afraid.

4

Lessons for Sau and Kar

A MONTH LATER Sau and Kar were back once more in the Village of Sixteen Peaks. Sau did not stay long, however, but soon returned to the tribes center in Dalat.

Kar was content to remain at home. Often he heard the villagers talking about how Sau had stopped the sorcerer's band, and every time he did, he flushed with pleasure. His older brother had asked him to go along to help thwart the plan and he complied. Wasn't he glad that he had done so?

Usually he obeyed Sau and everything turned out well. Yet there was one matter in which he still had not heeded his brother's advice— "Believe and follow the God of Heaven."

Kar grew more and more troubled. He felt that he should believe. Others in the village besides Sau were beginning to speak of how happy they were, now that they no longer feared the power of evil spirits. Kar wanted to believe, but the pressures on him not to believe were still great.

The old people—they were the ones who counted—still held to the ancient ways. That kept Kar back. It wasn't easy to turn from the spirits that one had known since childhood to a God one was just beginning to know.

He found it hard, too, to abandon the old customs that the God-Followers in the village were beginning to find distasteful. They were often right in their disapproval, he said to himself. But what, for instance, could one do about the time-honored ceremony of having one's front teeth sawed off by a notched ax as a preparation for marriage?

His brother Sau had not yet submitted to the ordeal when as a youth he went to live in Dalat. And when he came back to visit he reported that people in town wore their teeth—why shouldn't the tribesmen wear theirs?

The villagers had taunted Sau.

"You look like a dog," said an old uncle.

"A boy with his front teeth will never find a wife," observed a woman with an eligible daughter whom she would have liked to marry off.

Kar was crushed by the insults. He had held out since the years of his puberty, but now, at nearly twenty, he was afraid that what they said was true: Wearing his front teeth, he would never get a wife.

One day he decided to submit to the painful ordeal. On his way to the scene of the ritual he wished that Sau were not in Dalat, but in the village. On second thought, he was glad that Sau was away. Sau would talk him out of the sawing, as he had done other years. He would say that if God wanted Kar to have a wife, God would send him one.

That was all right for Sau to say for himself—perhaps God would send him a wife, although Kar could not possibly see how. As for himself, he didn't know what he could expect from God; the only thing he knew for certain was that tribespeople had their teeth sawed off.

Once more Sau left Dalat, and went back to the mountains to preach and teach. As he traveled, he heard of dark threats against him muttered by the python worshipers. But he was not afraid. He took his success in turning the band back from Dalat as a signal to redouble his efforts; God had granted the tribespeople a reprieve from sure, swift punishment and Sau did not want to fail them now. From village to village he went, among the people of his own tribe; these were called the Chil—the dwellers in the high mountains.

One of the settlements that Sau visited was Monkey Village, where he had lived as a boy. Now he found himself going back there again and again.

It was a young woman who drew him. He had known her since he was a boy. In fact, it was through his teaching that she had become a God-Follower. Her name was Drim. For a tribeswoman she was tall and large-boned. To Sau, this seemed only to enhance her attractiveness.

In his trips to her village he became more and more impressed with Drim. She was shy, and Sau thought her pretty. He felt that here was a woman who could take the trails in stride and who, when dedicated to a cause, would see it through without complaining.

For a long time Sau had wanted for a wife a woman who would accept his wanderings and his unrest, one who would share his vision and enthusiasm—and also one who would bear him many children.

Drim, he believed, was all that he had ever hoped for.

But he was not in a position to ask her to be his wife.

Among the tribespeople the girls did the choosing—or rather their mothers did. For generations it had been the custom for a mother to invite eligible young men to spend the night with her daughter. When the girl was large with child, the mother would pick from the lot of likely fathers the one she wanted most for a son-in-law.

In some instances the mother invited the youths and their parents to a feast, and the boy who found a brass ring at the bottom of his gourd of cloudy rice alcohol was thereby betrothed to the girl.

Negotiations preceded every marriage. The steps toward agreement, once taken, could not be annulled without a suit leading to considerable indemnity. Bringing a judgment against a neighbor was a favorite pastime of the mountain people. Sometimes the trial was held before the authorities, more often by tests of fire or water before fellow villagers. To avoid these costly judgments, the negotiators in a marriage contract dealt both skillfully and carefully. Each side held out for as much as the traffic would bear—why settle for three water buffalo and two baskets of unhusked rice when the figures might be pushed higher?

The time came when Sau asked an elder of Monkey Village to induce Drim's parents to seek him as their daughter's husband.

The elder, however, thought Sau's suit quite hopeless. "You have your teeth," he reminded him.

"Find out if she likes me—just a little," Sau pleaded. "Speak in my behalf."

One day Drim came with her mother and father to Sixteen Peaks to negotiate with Sau's relatives. Drim's parents indicated that they would ask for him, if his price was not too high. Sau himself stepped in and took over the palaver.

"The only dowry I want," he said, "is your daughter." At this Drim's mother regarded Sau suspiciously.

"I am a preacher for the God of Heaven," he explained. "I cannot come and live in your house and work for you as is the custom. I must go from village to village; I till my field only when I can. I am asking that your daughter be allowed to live where I live."

Drim's mother was undecided. To lose a daughter thus—while not gaining a son-in-law to work in her fields—was definitely not to her liking. Yet, she was poor, heavily in debt, so what could she offer to attract a young man to her household? Better to lose Drim than to keep her daughter at home without a husband.

Sau now moved to sway her to a decision. "I promise you this," he began. "When I am old and can no longer preach, I will come then to live in your village."

This was enough for Drim's mother—and because it was enough for her, it sufficed for the father, too. Since Sau had not demanded buffalo or rice or cloth—none of which they possessed—Drim's parents thought that his request, though unusual, was reasonable. After a year of betrothal, Drim could become his wife.

Sau and Drim then ate pork together before their relatives to seal their engagement. During the feast Sau learned for the first time that Drim had talked of him convincingly to persuade her parents to ask for him.

"You wanted me because we both are God-Followers?" Sau asked.

Drim nodded shyly. But there was something more. He teased her until she told him.

"I remember the first time you came to our village," Drim said. "From my mother's house I saw you come. You did not look like the other men. You wore clothes, and our men wore only loincloths. Your white shirt—I thought it was so pretty. And then you called all of us in the village together. You said you wanted to teach us.

"I knew you were different then," she went on. "But I knew it before I understood what you told us. I knew I wanted you when you first called us together. As you opened your mouth to speak I saw you had your teeth. They were like your shirt. And to wear your teeth though you were no longer a child—to do that, you had to be a man unlike our men."

One day about a year later when Sau was again at the tribes center in Dalat, he was pleasantly surprised to hear Grandfather say he was going out to visit villages in the mountains. Grandfather said

that as a result of Sau's warning, the French had adopted a new attitude toward the work of the missionaries. No longer were they confined to Dalat. The government had lifted the limits on their ministry
and was even encouraging them to spread the Gospel among the
tribespeople.

On one of his first journeys, Grandfather and his helpers were to
visit a small village not far from Sixteen Peaks. The express purpose
of the trip was to marry the young men whom the missionary had
taught at the tribes center to Christian girls. But the visit would also
give Grandfather the opportunity to meet people whom he had never
seen, but who worshiped the same God.

At the edge of the village was a swift, clear mountain stream.
Before Grandfather could cross it, he and his party were met on the
near bank by Sau and a crowd of singing villagers.

This was the greatest welcome the visitors had ever experienced.
But even the excited chatter in an unfamiliar dialect, and the rhythmic
beat of gongs, could not distract Grandfather's attention from a tiny
bamboo building at the far end of the village. Here the God-Followers
had built their own chapel! It appeared to be filled and overflowing
with people awaiting their arrival. From within came the strains of a
hymn he had taught his students at the tribes center. As he entered,
he saw a number of familiar faces; but there were many more he did
not know.

"It's true!" Jackson exclaimed. "Away back here in the mountains,
these people know God." He was finally allowing himself to believe
his most cherished dream.

He questioned those who waited to shake his hand as to how
they had become believers.

"Sau taught me in my village," one young man replied.

The others told similar stories. Jackson bowed his head—this was
God's doing, and he was awed and grateful. During the years he had
not been allowed to go beyond Dalat, he taught. Lydia and K'Sol and
Tam, his Annamese helper, had taught; and the men who gathered
at the evening fires or in the classroom had accepted the teaching
and returned to the mountains to spread the Gospel.

If there were a dozen believers living in this one village, how
many God-Followers were scattered throughout the province?

Sau was overjoyed at Grandfather's coming. To Sau, the occasion
was an opportunity to tell the pagans here about the God of Heaven.

To hear Sau witness of Christ to the unbelievers was to wonder
if he'd forgotten that this was the day of his marriage. But Sau had
not forgotten. He himself went from house to house to make sure that
no one missed the ceremony. So many sought to get into the little
chapel that the crowd, at Grandfather's suggestion, was moved out of
the building to the bank of the stream. Before fifty-odd villagers
seated or squatting, Sau walked solemnly with Drim at his side from
the chapel to stand before Grandfather.

Sau smiled a bit nervously. He wore an old and slightly worn but
recently washed suit. His hands were shoved into the jacket pockets.
In one pocket his fingers traced the carvings on a bracelet he had
brought to the wedding. His tie choked him a little, but whether it
was this or the occasion that caused the flush on his face, he was
not quite certain.

In all her simplicity Drim appeared to Sau as a beautiful bride.
The dark hue of her homespun skirt contrasted to the whiteness of
the blouse, which she had purchased at the market long ago and
saved for her marriage. She had drawn her heavy black hair into a
bun and covered it with a simple white headcloth. To Sau, this
emphasized the nobility of her expression. Others may have thought
that her knitted brow and the deep lines that ran from the corners
of her eyes showed concern over this step she was taking; Sau regarded these signs as the marks of a woman determined to do the
will of God.

Grandfather's voice aroused him from his reverie. He was now
asking Sau something that demanded all his attention.

"Will you love and protect Drim and always be faithful to her?"
Grandfather was saying, improvising the vows since he had forgotten
to bring his marriage book.

"Yes, yes," Sau quickly replied, making the matter of a spoken
vow seem quite unnecessary.

Grandfather then asked Drim if she would have Sau as her husband. There was a pause. Intently, the crowd awaited her answer.
Instead, they heard only the sound of the water rushing past the
stones in the stream. Grandfather looked up sharply at Drim. Sau
cocked his head toward her. Why didn't she respond? But if others
were anxious, Drim was not. She was reflecting with some delibera-
tion. When the full meaning of Grandfather's words sank in, she
quietly said, "Yes, I will have him."

Her answer brought a sigh of relief from the onlookers. The service moved on. Grandfather regarded them seriously.

"You know that God is looking down from Heaven," he reminded them. Both nodded.

The missionary then prayed, and in his prayer said it was God, not man, who was joining Sau and Drim. When he finished he smiled at the couple, his severity completely vanished.

"Now for the bracelets," he said.

Sau drew from his pocket the one he had brought for Drim. She had tucked a plain brass wrist piece in the waist of her skirt; now she took it out. They exchanged bracelets. Tam, who was standing by ready to assist if needed, stepped forward with a strand of bright colored beads. These he placed around the neck of the shy but now happy bride.

The rites were similar for each of the other couples. Then the God-Followers killed a pig and staked it over a fire in preparation for the feast.

They invited the pagans of the village to eat with them. These unbelievers feasted with gusto; at the same time they shook their heads querulously. What kind of a wedding celebration was this?

"There is no rice wine," a man complained to his friend.

"And they do not call the spirits to help us eat," the friend observed.

Such oversights, the two agreed, were not only strange but portended ill for the future.

While others ate, Sau and Drim withdrew from the crowd and slipped into a house further to symbolize their union before the village elder. From a single bowl which he held before them, they both ate handfuls of rice. From that time on, each was to call the other *minoi*. *Minoi* meant "myself"—the two were now one—and the responsibility that this engendered brought a closeness, though not familiarity, to their relationship.

In a few days Sau walked with his bride to Sixteen Peaks.

Their appearance created something of a stir, since his marriage had brought a new daughter, not a son, into the village. But the house to which Sau brought Drim caused even more talk.

Standing higher off the ground than the others, Sau's was the only one in the village to have windows. Unlike the houses of Sau's neighbors, it was not intended as a dwelling for an entire clan, although he made it known that visitors were always welcome. Drim liked it. She was especially proud of the benches and a table her husband had carved from logs to make their living easier.

"How do you sit on your bench?" the villagers who knew nothing of town ways asked as they crowded in. But when Sau invited them to try the benches, they excused themselves by saying, "Oh, we'd rather sit on our mats on the floor."

Sau explained to those who came that when one had grown accustomed to sitting on chairs, it was hard to get used to sitting cross-legged once more.

If Sau was not to live in a grand villa in Dalat, he was determined at least that his house in the mountains should be as fine as he could make it.

At one end of the big room he had hung walls of woven bamboo to form two smaller rooms. Bedrooms, he called them—one for his wife and himself, and one for guests. Back in Dalat, Grandfather had promised that someday he and Grandmother would come. Sau wanted to be ready to receive them.

Sau decorated his table and walls with orchids. He made a hatrack out of the antlers of a deer. Visitors also found a curious assortment of items he had brought home at one time or another from the market in Dalat: a metal pitcher to take the place of a water gourd; an oil lamp to supplement the flickering light of the cooking fire; a calendar with beautiful pictures to brighten a wall.

He had earned the price of every possession. No one matched his enterprise in working to buy what he needed.

Between his long trips for preaching and teaching, he worked hard in the fields at Sixteen Peaks. Never idle for so much as half an hour, he constantly looked for things to do. Others might rest in the middle of the day, the only time the sun warmed the mountains, but Sau did not. He would put the time to good use by making a squirrel trap or by memorizing the words of a neighboring tribe's dialect.

He was not content to reap the meager harvests that his fellow villagers accepted as their fate. He felt driven to accumulate possessions. The greater his wealth, he thought, the greater the evidence of God's ability to provide.

"Clear more fields and plant more corn and rice, and your harvest will be more bountiful," he counseled the God-Followers.

E

He knew that if a believer lacked food or a good house or tools, those who still refused to believe would be only too quick to say:

"So, your God is not a good one to serve."

Yet, as time went on, Sau seemed to care more about what people thought of him than what they thought of God. At times he was no longer satisfied with having his needs provided for, but was anxious, instead, for abundance.

At the same time, however, Sau was forever giving of himself. He was always ready to help someone raise a house, was always the one to come in the middle of the night to pray for a sick child.

Time after time Sau and Drim walked the trail to Dalat. On each trip his appetite for new things increased. But he tried hard not to let this obsession rule his life. Every time he saw something beyond his means, he prayed that he not become envious.

"God in God's own time will give me things of my own," he said to reassure himself.

There was nothing that Sau would rather do than preach. He knew if he were to preach well, he would have to study hard every chance he got. Therefore, whenever he was at the tribes center he spent long hours under the teaching of Grandmother and Grandfather and of Tam and K'Sol. He was too restless to sit long at a desk. But Sau could not remain away from the trail for more than a few weeks at a time. When he was back in the mountains telling people about the God of Heaven, Dalat and its splendors would gradually fade.

In many ways Sau was still an apprentice. He was grateful to those who taught him. Once he accompanied Grandfather and Tam and K'Sol on a teaching trip through the land of K'Sol's people, who were called the Sre tribe.

The Sre tribe lived on a flat plain. They planted their rice in flooded fields. For this reason it tasted different from mountain rice. Sau did not like wet rice and spoke disparagingly of it to K'Sol. His attitude disturbed K'Sol.

"Keep your mind open to new people, new ways," K'Sol advised Sau one night as they sat around their campfire. He confirmed what he said by his actions. At the moment he was practicing his most recently acquired skill. He was knitting a sweater for his wife.

"Know the Bible well," he counseled further.

K'Sol had made a study of Old Testament characters. The law and the prophets were not yet translated into the tribal tongue, but he had read about them in the Annamese Bible. K'Sol observed that God brought blessing on His children when they were obedient and punished them when they were wicked. He believed God would do the same to his own generation. Daniel was preserved in the den of hungry lions and the three Hebrew children lived in the fiery furnace because they trusted in the God of Heaven, he reminded Sau. But Nebuchadnezzar was driven to dwell with the beasts and eat grass as an ox because of his pride.

K'Sol made sure that Sau got the point.

Heaven? K'Sol delighted in talking about it. He was sure it was a place of grandeur. Once he had gone to Saigon. He saw a large French store that by day he thought was magnificent, but that by night was even more amazing. For a long while he gazed at the brilliantly lighted display windows. One window containing jewels made his eyes dance.

"Heaven . . ." the little man said at their campfire one night, rolling back his head and looking to the stars while groping for fitting words, ". . . Heaven is better than—than Charnier's Store!"

On trips, at the tribes center, or wherever they were together, Sau learned much from K'Sol. He did all that K'Sol advised, and more.

Back among his own tribe he frequently went to new places that had not yet heard about the Spirit of the Skies. But he was also faithful to the old places and went back often to teach them over and over. Often he became discouraged because converts did not come as fast as he hoped they would.

"I tell them about God, but they don't seem to understand," he said to himself wearily one day. "And if they do understand, they refuse to accept God."

Some days he felt very tired from all his walking the trails, his frequent teaching, his unending work. It was not that he felt like giving up. Rather he chafed with impatience over the slowness of others to respond.

But there was a bright spot in Sau's life these days. Kar had finally decided it was the God of Heaven he wanted to serve.

"God gave my brother a wife," Kar had mused. To him, this was accomplishing the impossible—to provide a wife for one who had flouted their teeth-sawing custom. If God could help Sau that way, could God just possibly help Kar?

For many years Sau had seen much in Kar that God could use. His brother had courage; he was willing, even eager, to tackle the hard tasks; he hung on tenaciously until a job was done. For a long time Sau taught him the Gospel without any visible response. Then one day Kar said to him:

"I see it!"

And he did. Like Sau before him, he had developed a delicious ear for the words of God.

Almost from the moment he became a believer Kar began to preach. His first messages were brief and very simple.

"God is good," he said from Sau's pulpit in the village chapel one day. "I was not good. But Jesus died because I was not good. God said, 'That's enough dying for sin.' Now I have God's goodness in me."

But his new life was not easy for Kar. People pointed out to him that he was not much more than a boy. What did he know about life that he could teach *them?* Not long before, Kar himself had drunk with them at the spirit feasts. Did he know the God of Heaven so very well?

They compared him with Sau, and by the comparison Kar suffered. But his older brother encouraged him. Sau told him to listen to God, not to the old people who disparaged him or to the young ones who liked to tease him.

Three years after Sau's marriage Kar found a girl he wanted to be his wife. She was one of the God-Followers of his own village. He asked Sau to negotiate with the girl's parents. He needn't have asked. Sau had already spoken with the parents—and put in a good word on Kar's behalf.

Her name was Gien. A small woman, she was not physically strong. But she had an inner fire that sustained her. She also possessed initiative, was a good organizer, and was self-denying. More than once after she married Kar did Gien preach in the thatched chapel when both Sau and Kar were away.

A few months after their first child was born, Kar stood watching Gien trample the stalks of rice to thresh it, then hull it with pestle and mortar. All the while she carried her baby in a blanket tied to her back. Not by having your teeth hacked out did you get such a wonderful wife, he told himself. No, this kind came by the providence of God—and, he also had to admit, by the plain but forgivable

matchmaking of an older brother. Kar wondered if any other man
could be so happy. He did not know that trying times were just ahead.

One evening Sau reminded his brother that once he had said he
would go to Grandfather's school after Sau taught him all that he
was able.

"I am going back there in two weeks to learn more myself," Sau
said. "I think that this time you should come with me."

Kar hesitated. He wanted to go, but he had no money for the
food needed to sustain himself in the city. He talked it over with
Gien.

"It will take two hundred piasters," he said. He thought it was
useless to consider going. Not Gien. She, no less than Sau, wanted
Kar to study. She thought it over. Then one night, when she was
chasing their pig home from the forest, she came upon the answer.

"Sell the pig," she said to Kar. "Ask two hundred piasters for
it." She made it sound so simple, which it proved to be.

Kar sold the pig and got the money. Then, with Sau and Drim
and his brother's two small sons, he walked to the tribes center in
Dalat. He had money in his pocket and determination in his heart.

The school had grown since Sau's first instruction by the missionary
and K'Sol. New buildings sprang up, and in one of them the students
ate. Krong, an older student who helped turn back the python
marchers, was in charge of the men who earned part of their keep
by working in the dining room and kitchen. Kar was assigned to
Krong's crew. He found him a hard master.

On the first day, after dinner, Kar was going from the dining room
to the kitchen house with his rice bowl and spoon.

"Idiot! Come here!" Krong called to him.

Kar laid his bowl down on a table, then went outside to Krong.
The latter stood by a row of big glazed green jars that lined a wall
of the building, and stared at him haughtily.

"Your brother tells me you can't read," Krong snapped.

"It's true," Kar confessed, "but I've come to learn."

"For what reason?" asked Krong disdainfully. He seemed to have
forgotten that he himself was little more than an ignorant savage just
a few years before. "How can God use anyone so stupid?"

It was his way of making the new men aware that he was boss.
He pointed to the jars—there must have been a half dozen.

"Those are water jars. Every day you will carry water from the cistern and fill each jar to the top before you eat your dinner," Krong ordered.

Kar thanked Krong quietly for giving him the task. He was glad to be in school, and this was a part of school.

The next day he discovered just how great the chore was.

To supply water for the whole school meant making many trips to the cistern. Kar did it without complaining, even though he missed the big main meal at noon. He rose early next morning to start on his task before classes. Still, he couldn't finish by dinnertime. Again he went without eating.

Hungry and disappointed, Kar did poorly in his studies. By the end of the first week he was thoroughly discouraged. Early one morning he slipped out of the dormitory and headed for the path to Sixteen Peaks.

When Sau did not see his brother at morning devotions, he became suspicious. He ran after him. He caught up with Kar while he was still on the road.

"Why have you run away?" Sau asked sternly.

"It is so hard," replied Kar, hanging his head.

"Of course it is hard." Sau spoke angrily. He stood between his brother and the path to home, and it was plain that if he could not turn Kar around with words he would attempt it bodily.

"Hard?" Sau went on. "Do you think that after working with a shoulder ax I found it easy to hold a pencil? Do you suppose that I got a delicious ear for God's words without working at it?"

He would not hear of Kar's quitting. He marched him back to Dalat as if Kar were his little son rather than a brother who stood taller than he.

At the tribes center Sau's wife Drim was working in the kitchen to help prepare the student meals. One day she noticed that her young brother-in-law did not eat with the rest. When he finished filling the water jars she called him aside.

"Would you like a bowl of rice and vegetables?" she asked.

Would he! Three times he emptied the biggest rice bowl in the kitchen.

Every day after that Drim and the other women held out food for Kar. And when they could find the time they helped him carry the water. One day Drim told Sau how hard Krong was making it for Kar.

"So that is why he ran away," Sau said, understanding Kar's discouragement for the first time.

"You should do something to help him," Drim suggested.

He felt that he should. Sau had been angry at his brother for leaving. But his flareups never lasted long, nor was he one to hold a grudge. His irritation melted in a rush of sympathy for Kar. His feeling went very deep. It was he who had brought his younger brother to this place—and for what? To be picked on and misused, as it had turned out. He grew angry again, this time at the one who had dared treat his beloved brother so. He wanted to bring Krong up before Grandfather or K'Sol for judgment. He thought for several minutes how he might do it. Then once again his anger left him. He shook his head, and to Drim said "No."

In his heart was an ache—for Kar and for Krong.

Sau would find it difficult to keep silent when the injustice was so flagrant. It would take all his restraint to stand by and observe in silence all the slights Kar was enduring that he had not noticed before.

But Sau could not fight his brother's battles for him, especially when those battles were spiritual. Spiritual? Yes, Kar had to learn to lean on God for strength, not on the resources of an older brother.

5

No More the Old Days

Just over beyond the mountains which surrounded Sixteen Peaks lived the Tring. They were the most difficult of all the mountain tribes that Sau had tried to reach. They were shy. When strangers approached they scurried into the forest. The Tring were the poorest, most fear-ridden tribe of all. If Sau's people often went hungry, the Tring lived always on the edge of starvation.

They did not live in villages.

The spirits that ruled them forbade one family to dip water from another's source; one of them could not even live across the stream from an in-law. So Tring houses were spotted sparsely for long distances along the mountain rivers, each a desolate picture of isolation.

Clinging to the steep, stony sides of mountains for mere existence, the Tring shivered in the ceaseless cold of the wind. Often gusts broke down the corn before it could come into ear. The wet monsoon blew when they needed it to be dry, and when it was dry for too long they suffered from the drought.

The demons, too, kept them hungry. If a man went to his field in the morning and found dew on the ground, he returned home without working that day to avoid a curse.

If fortune kept him away from his field beyond the planting season—well, it was evident that the spirits did not want him to find his food in such an easy way.

And if he did plant, he was careful not to plant enough to satisfy his needs. The spirits always demanded of him that he search in the forest for roots and leaves to eke out his diet. For this reason he was inclined to plant just enough mountain rice to keep his alcohol jars full.

Sau and Kar's father had been a Tring. As a boy of fourteen, he was one day on the border between the Tring and a neighboring tribe, the Chil. A band of Chil men, seeing him alone, captured him; he would make a suitable husband, they thought, for one of the girls in their village. Before getting back to their side, they encountered the young man's friends. To avoid a fight, the Chil invited the Tring to eat a pig with them and offered a dowry of brass gongs, which according to their calculations were worth at least three water buffalo.

The Tring accepted the offer, so he was taken, against his will, to Monkey Village, the home of the Chil. For two days and two nights he refused to eat, but hunger finally forced him to agree to marry. Thus he became a Chil. From that union issued Sau and Kar and a half-dozen other children, most of whom died in the course of time.

Sau had visited the Tring often on his preaching missions, living first with one family, then another, in his effort to free them from the grip of their oppressive superstition.

Only one out of so many, a thin, sad-eyed lad of eight named Thanh, seemed to grasp what Sau taught. Once, between Sau's visits, the boy became deathly ill. Sau learned on his next trip that Thanh had refused to let his mother call in the sorcerer.

"The God of Heaven will heal me, not the sacrifice demanded by the sorcerer," the boy had said. And summoning strength to shake his tiny fist, he warned:

"If the sorcerer comes I will take a stick and hit him on the head."

Thanh's mother, fearing her son meant what he said, did not summon the sorcerer. She knew that if offended, he could bring untold evil on her house.

Sau hoped that soon other Tring would come to believe with as much earnestness as Thanh. But for several years he was not to know. The world was suddenly at war.

Small, polite soldiers—the Japanese—had been in the tribesmen's country for over a year. Their presence seemed to make little difference until a few days before Christmas, 1941, when the Japanese told the missionaries they could not leave their houses. Two years later the Japanese took the Americans away, and interned them in a city on the Mekong Delta.

For a while in the absence of the Jacksons, Tam and other Annamese Christians kept the tribes center open. Then by order of the Japanese they, too, had to leave. Sau and the other God-Followers among the tribes were left entirely on their own.

Sau kept on going to the villages as often as he could. His white shirts wore out and the clothing that remained was little more than rags. Contact with America had been cut off, and the mail that brought money to support tribal preachers came no longer. Like others, Sau had to depend on his rice field and his skill as a hunter to live.

As conditions grew worse, Sau could not be gone long from Drim his wife and their two growing sons. Places which he used to frequent he now had to pass up altogether.

But fields and forests and the presence of foreign soldiers were not all that interfered with Sau's preaching at this time.

One day he arrived back from a short stay in Dalat and disclosed to friends congregated before his house that he had taken a job with the government.

"They asked me to work for them," he said, thinking his people would like to know.

"I thought you worked for God," said a puzzled old uncle.

"I do," Sau assured him. "I'm a preacher—as always. But I also help the *capitaine* in Dalat."

"We know what you do for God," a woman said. "We don't know what you do for the Frenchman."

"I tell the *capitaine* if there is much sickness in the mountain villages. And if he has a message for the tribespeople, I put it in our language. Then I bring the message back to the villages—though I have had none to deliver as yet," he said.

"Why do you work for the government?" his brother Kar asked.

"They need a tribesman who can speak their language," he replied. "And they pay me. I am able to buy more things at the market for my wife and my boys."

He was carrying a bundle on his shoulders. He turned to go up the notched pole to his house; he indicated that when he came out he would let them see what was in the bundle. He soon emerged wearing the white trousers and long, flowered tunic of an Annamese.

"Ohhhh!" the people cried, greatly impressed.

Sau smiled as he came slowly down the notched pole so that they could have a good look at his new costume.

"This the *capitaine* gave me," he said proudly. The villagers pressed around to feel its softness.

"How pretty!" said one. "Get some like that for us."

Yes, it was pretty, Sau said to himself. Yet, he didn't feel right wearing it. Nor did he feel comfortable about the money he was to be paid in Dalat. As he put on his old familiar clothes he said to himself that he ought not to be working for the government.

Oh, there was nothing wrong with the job. He would be helping the tribespeople, wouldn't he? The Japanese, though they now ruled the country, had so far left the French in charge of many things, and the French were showing some interest in improving the lot of the mountain people in Dalat's province.

But Sau worked for God. He couldn't find time enough to do all that God wanted him to do. And here he was at the same time trying to serve another master.

Sau came to a sudden decision. He just wouldn't do it any longer.

He would miss the fine clothes and the other things he could buy. But the next time he went to Dalat he would ask to be excused.

Some weeks later he stood in the *capitaine's* office. He made his request for dismissal. The government, however, had not filled the post of tribes adviser hastily. Sau was told he would not be allowed to quit.

"But, *m'sieur le capitaine*," Sau pleaded. "I am a preacher of the Gospel. My heart is only for my preaching."

The officer shook his head stubbornly. Sau sank to his knees. He sobbed. He told God (and since Sau spoke in French the *capitaine* could listen if he liked) that he was only good for preaching.

The officer was finally convinced he had lost his man. Reluctantly, he released him.

With no missionary there in those years to comfort in sorrow and advise with problems, the God-Followers leaned more heavily on God, and this was good. Still, they sorely felt the need of the missionaries' teaching. So it was a happy day when the Japanese finally went home and by their going the missionaries were able to return. Back came the Jacksons and the faithful Annamese. Everyone said that soon it would be like old days again. But they were wrong.

Now the jungle trails took on a danger that had not existed before. A person could be on his way to market only to be stopped by strange men who took from him his rice or mushrooms or mountain

fruit. For a long time Sau did not understand. But one day he thought
he was beginning to grasp the reasons for this peril.

The Japanese had suffered defeat in a war—not in Sau's land,
where there were only skirmishes with the French. But after they removed the Americans, and later the French, to places of imprison-
ment, they themselves were beaten in neighboring lands and withdrew
to their islands up north.

The French then came back to rule Indo-China. They, too, thought
the old days had returned. They found however, a changed colony;
the natives they once governed did not want them back. The seeds of
discontent had long been nurtured; perhaps they had been planted
with the python worship.

During Japanese occupation and France's absence the people's
hunger for independence had grown. Indeed, it was said by many that
the Japanese had left two gifts behind when they went home: the
lovely cherry trees that now blossomed in Dalat, and the kindled
yearning for self-government.

Sau wanted his country to be free. But he wasn't sure who was
going to win its freedom. The Annamese seemed bitterly divided—
only one thing was certain: they were not to be called Annamese
anymore. They insisted on this.

"That's the name the conquerors gave us," they reminded each
other. Sau heard men on the streets of Dalat proclaim themselves
"citizens of Viet Nam." The name had come down from ancient
days.

These people tolerated the French, who were trying to pick up the
pieces and in places succeeding very well, though the Vietnamese
chafed to be free of them.

There were some who felt even more strongly about the French.
They went by the name of Viet Minh, and thought the only good
Frenchman was a dead Frenchman. Pledging themselves to drive
France from the land, they lurked in the forest, foraged for food,
struck lightning blows at settlements they could not control.

The tribesmen observed this strange struggle between the Viet
Minh and the French and between the "VM" and the rest of the
Vietnamese. They had every reason to remain aloof. If the French
had not treated them well, had the yellow man done any better? Yet
even in their mountains they could not help getting caught up in
the bitter conflict. Sometimes in walking the trail one would en-

counter a band of the Viet Minh, and at such time one never knew what to expect.

It was this way when one day in 1947 Sau suddenly came on two strangers in the path.

He was far from home, far from any village that he knew, and the trail here ran through dense jungle. The sun was straight overhead, but that made little difference under the nearly solid canopy of vegetation. It was so dim that Sau had come within fifty paces of the men before he saw that they bore weapons.

Ordinarily such a discovery might have made him hide off the path, but they had seen him. One had even called out to him. He continued on toward them.

Before he could see them plainly, one of the men slipped into the underbrush and out of sight. The one remaining, he could now tell, carried a gun on his hip as well as a rifle. Sau noticed that he was an Annamese—he corrected himself—a Vietnamese, maybe one of the Viet Minh.

The man wore ill-fitting long black trousers, and the military jacket of a French legionnaire. His head was bare; his feet were lost in oversized combat boots. Despite these incongruities, Sau thought he appeared rather forceful. Maybe it was his face. He was staring hard at Sau.

Sau greeted him. The man replied in a friendly manner. This surprised Sau, so he spoke again:

"Are you going to Lieng Bong?" That village was Sau's destination.

"No," the man said tersely.

"To Set Meh?" It was the village from which Sau had come.

"No."

Sau wasn't sure now that the encounter would be friendly. Here was a man with two guns in the middle of the forest who was evidently going no place. Sau wondered why.

It became the stranger's turn to put the questions.

"Do others follow you?" he asked. Sau hesitated, then slowly shook his head.

"I, too, am alone," he said. Why did he say that? Hadn't Sau seen that there were two at first and that one dropped away into the brush? He looked at the spot where the second man had left the path. Only undisturbed ferns and vines were there now. Yet he

sensed that from somewhere in that thick cover a pair of eyes
watched him closely, and that most likely the barrel of a gun was
pointed at his head.

"You eat well," the one in the path said to Sau.

"We have our good crops and bad."

"You have good ones—"

"And bad ones."

"Your people are poor?"

"We eat—if not rice, the roots and leaves that God provides in
the forest for anyone willing to gather them."

"Wouldn't you like to own a rice house overflowing with grain?"
the stranger asked, and Sau wondered how the man had been able
to read his thoughts.

"I would like that, yes," Sau replied.

"And a horse so you would not have to walk the trail?"

"Yes," Sau laughed lightly. "A horse, too—and one of the pony
carts in Dalat."

"These things someday our leader will bring us," the man said in
a serious yet confident tone. "Do you know our leader?"

"No, I don't know him," Sau said.

"He is Ho Chi Minh."

"Ho Chi Minh I have heard of—a little," said Sau. "The Viet
Minh—you are of the Viet Minh?"

"What do you think of our leader?"

"I think," Sau replied, "that if Ong Minh obeyed the God of
Heaven much blessing could come to our land through him."

Sau took a step, as though he would go on. The man grabbed
Sau's arm.

"Wait," he said roughly. "I invite you to stay."

"I am on my way to the village of Lieng Bong."

"I ask you to help our cause."

"I cannot. I am a preacher for the God of Heaven."

The man dropped Sau's arm, but Sau made no further move to
go on. He had to hear out this member of the Viet Minh guerrillas.

"I invite you," said the man whose face now pushed close to Sau's,
"to help us win our struggle."

"I have no gun," Sau said.

"But you have food."

"We have good crops and bad. I have already told you."

"We ask only for what you can supply."

"If a strong wind blows and our rice and corn fall down, what can we give you?"

"We will be the judge of that. Just tell your people to be ready." With that the man turned and walked away from Sau. Sau went on, not daring to look behind him.

So this was what it was like to meet the guerrillas in a forest path! It seemed that he could almost feel a bullet slamming into the back of his brain. But the more ground he covered, slowly at first, then with quickened pace, the safer he felt. Then he decided he didn't really feel safe at all.

He didn't feel safe because he felt his people were not safe. The man had not actually threatened him. But trouble clearly lay ahead.

Putting the recent encounter out of his mind as perhaps a menace more fancied than real, Sau hit trail after trail. Once again American money was coming to help the tribal preachers buy food for their families, so Sau was able to cut down on the size of his field. Since his people were beginning to help him farm, he now had more time and was able to reach out farther in his effort to evangelize.

In many Chil villages the people looked forward to his coming. Often they recognized him while he still walked the path on a mountain slope opposite theirs. They couldn't always tell by his shirt nowadays—he was glad to get whatever mission or market had to offer, and when there was a choice, he usually picked red or something with stripes. The people could, however, recognize him by the vigor of his stride; and whether he came at a lope or bounding gait, he was always energetic.

Everywhere he went he played with the children, making tops for them to spin or teaching them games of skill. He helped the parents with house-building or with planting; he fished with them; he often sat in judgment on the disputes they brought before him. At night as the men sat on their haunches around the clay-box fires in their longhouses and rocked on their heels and smoked, he spoke to them of God.

"If Christ comes to live in your hearts," he said to them often, "your fear of evil spirits will be driven out."

He spoke of a life after they would die. The part about Heaven was new to them. They knew about Hell—weren't they going there someday? They hated the prospect, but it did not change their solid conviction. All the tribesmen were doomed. For that despised journey into the ground they worked to gain strength and wealth and power so they might not go unprepared.

When a man had acquired some of these benefits, however, along would come the sorcerer with his pronouncement of dire consequences if the man did not give all he possessed in sacrifice. Many a soul had been left without hope.

"I owe the spirits thirteen buffalo," a villager said one night to Sau. He fingered the brass bracelet on his arm. He meant that he had been ordered to sacrifice that many, but not having the buffalo, had notched his bracelet as a promise to the spirits to do so.

Others complained to him of their indebtedness to neighbors. An invitation to a sacrifice feast carried with it the obligation to give a feast in return. More than one child had been sold as a slave to pay off his father's debt for such feasts.

"I have thought," said a young man who had listened intently to Sau's message, "that if I become a believer in the God of Heaven I may escape my debt."

Sau quickly sought to correct his impression.

"To become a God-Follower releases you from the power of the evil spirits," he said. "It does not cancel your debt to a neighbor."

How, then, could they not sacrifice and yet pay their creditors what they owed them?

"Do you owe a buffalo?" Sau asked. "Work hard and be frugal and buy one. Then pay your debt by giving a feast. But at that feast do not call on the spirits."

After he had heard Sau's words, turning to God did not seem quite so attractive to the young questioner.

By this time most of the people of Sixteen Peaks were God-Followers. Sau influenced the young men there as K'Sol influenced him. Among them was a young Chil named Doi, reared among the Tring, who came back to visit his own people and was impressed by the good life he saw around him. Doi noticed that Sau had given up the multitude of spirits for the one Spirit of the Skies and because of it, no longer cringed when the devil bird hooted its death warning deep in the forest at night. Quiet and reflective, Doi wanted to be like Sau, who was always smiling and free from fear; he was overjoyed when Sau told him that he could be.

Two other young boys, both curly-haired and with quick wit and eagerness to serve the God of Heaven, often accompanied Sau on his trips. Their names were Sieng and Jao.

Kar, who had come a long way in his faith, caught something of his brother's vision of evangelizing pagan villages.

He had once gone with Sau to the Tring people after the way opened again to make that long trek. The trip was a sad experience for Sau; he found that in his absence during Japanese occupation the boy Thanh had bowed to the pressure of his tribe and returned to spirit worship.

Now Sau and Kar were once more on their way to the Tring. Starting out, they had to grope their way through a cloud. In this wet, blinding blanket they inched along, with Kar going first. More and more he was taking the lead these days in the church, in their village, wherever God-Followers congregated.

Kar by nature was jolly. Delivered from the inhibitions with which fear had shackled him, he became a radiant person. People liked him. They liked his ability to organize, to encourage them in finishing a task, to raise their spirits. Like Sau, Kar had quite a way with people. And Sau was glad that he did.

Now as they walked through this milky vapor talking of the Tring and of Sau's many visits to them, Kar stopped abruptly in the trail. Turning, he spoke as if suddenly inspired:

"Older brother, I have a feeling. I feel God would have me preach to the people of our father."

Sau thought Kar meant he would help do the preaching on this trip. "Of course, you will help me preach," he said. "There are more houses up and down the streams than even the two of us can reach while there."

"I do not mean on this trip only," Kar went on. "I mean I want to make my home among the Tring. I want to be there to teach them every day."

For a moment Sau was overwhelmed. He had hoped that someday Kar would carry on the work of teaching the Tring, although he wanted the Spirit of God, not himself, to prompt Kar. For weeks a plan by which he himself would reach still other people had been forming in his head. But there were always the Tring to care for— and now Kar had volunteered to do this job.

F

Sau felt like shouting; instead, he said quietly:

"You must be very sure of what you propose. You have a wife and young ones to think of."

"My wife will come with me," Kar replied. He said it with assurance. Why would she not come? She had encouraged him to leave their village to go to school in Dalat. She shared his growing concern for the unhappy souls around them.

On the second day the mist burned off; the sun shone brightly until the brothers entered a horseshoe gorge. The trail through the gorge led straight to the base of a rock that was bigger than a village longhouse. There was no other way that one could go. On either side the precipices were steeper still.

The rock itself resembled the wrinkled hide of an old elephant. On the higher ground above it a few tall trees grew, like hair on the head of a giant. From these trees long ropes of woody vine trailed against the face of the rock. Without them no one could mount to resume his journey at the top. Even so, few travelers were willing to risk the hand-over-hand climb that was inescapable.

"Turn back!" the rock seemed to cry out to any who wished to go to the Tring. And most people did turn back. The Tring believed a spirit lived in the rock. Thus it was both a natural and supernatural barrier between the tribe and the outer world.

On their last trip Sau and he had mounted the rock with difficulty, but they made their way over. Now that Kar had committed his wife to coming, however, he imagined the rock to have grown. It was as though the Devil stood on top to push them back down and keep them from bringing the Gospel in.

The brothers clutched the vines, again hoisting themselves and their baskets up the face of the rock. As they rested at the summit, Sau asked Kar once more if he was sure he wanted to bring his wife.

"She will come," said Kar, breathing heavily from the ordeal. "The way will be hard, but she has heard how sadly the Tring live."

Early on the third day they saw from a mountain peak a number of squat, disheveled houses dotting the slope before them. These were the dwellings of the Tring. They reached the first one shortly after sunup. There they found a sacrifice about to begin.

In the small clearing in front of the house—the only near-level spot around—a water buffalo stood docilely. It seemed not to mind the garlanded vine that laced it by the nostrils to a rack of strong logs. At the moment it appeared oblivious to a score of men and women fifteen paces away; and they, occupied by their alcohol jars, gave the beast no more notice than if it were grazing in last year's cornfield.

Sau and Kar dropped their baskets near a bamboo pole that towered over the house. The pole was the sacrificial mast. Carvings of deer, scorpion, peacock, and jecko lizard—so named from the noise it made—decorated the top, from which frayed bamboo also waved in the wind as a visual attraction to the spirits. Halfway up the shaft hung the skull of the last sacrificed buffalo. The skull of the creature tied to the rack would, before evening, be picked clean as if by vultures, and also be attached to the pole.

Six young men stood at the doorway of the house, rolling a throbbing rhythm from their gongs. They looked tired. All through the night they had been calling the spirits by their beat; only the ecstatic cadence and the fire of the rice drink kept them from falling in exhaustion.

Those at the jars had consumed a great deal of drink, yet there was much still before them. They stayed faithful to the liquor until someone (perhaps an old crone at the edge of the circle) signaled for the slaughter of the beast to begin.

A group of children wearing only ropes of beads ran from the house to dance crazily before the buffalo. Then grown men joined them in tantalizing the animal. From the house other men brought a big deerskin drum, adding its rumble to the sound of the gongs. With all this commotion, the spirits would not be long in gathering!

Suddenly one man brandished a long-bladed knife. His action sent the others scattering. He was thus left free to torment the beast by himself, which he did until his thrusts and parries ended in hamstringing the buffalo. Men now sprang with long spears. One by one they sent the weapons home into the helpless, hulking creature, and then danced away to the rhythm of the drum and gongs.

With a sad groan the buffalo expired. Young women rushed to the carcass with gourd pans to catch the blood that already stained the stony ground a reddish brown. Others cut chunks of the meat and threw them on the fire. The blood was precious. It would be daubed on the drum, on the house, and on themselves. While still warm it would either be mixed with the chopped and now slightly cooked flesh or be drunk with their rice alcohol.

The blood was the essence of the sacrifice. In consuming it lay the hope of a few days' relief from the wicked designs of the spirits.

Sau picked up his basket again. "Come," he said to Kar. He knew these people would eat and drink all day and perhaps kill another beast the following morning, and the morning after that, and maybe another water buffalo for each day until the new moon.

He knew that for days the vilest of orgies would take place, that the cries of babies would go unheard, and that as the effect of the drink wore off sickness from the filth and from eating the almost raw meat would set in—and then hunger again, followed by quarrels and fear of the spirits.

Sau and Kar went down by way of a ravine and up a slope to the house of a family whom Sau had visited before. He arranged for Kar to stay there while he went a day farther to see Thanh and his widowed mother. He was eager to meet the boy again, hoping he might win him back from spirit worship.

"Maybe God can gain many Tring through Thanh," he said to Kar before parting.

But when he arrived at Thanh's house, he found a sharp stick planted in the path. This meant only one thing: Stay away! Someone in the house might have died or might be very ill. Sau hoped it wasn't Thanh. He called, and the boy came out.

Thanh was now quite a young man, as tall as Sau, though very thin and frail. He had lost none of the sensitive bearing that marked him as a youngster.

He appeared more dispirited than Sau had ever seen him. "Oh, if I could only have him for a while," Sau thought, "to teach him, to cheer him, to help him see that God can lift his sad, troubled soul."

Thanh's face brightened when he saw Sau. He hurried past the pointed stick and grasped his mentor's hand. For some time they stood talking, the one dressed neatly despite his long trip, and with a look of confidence on his face, the other shivering in the barest fragment of a blanket and with the look of fear in his eyes.

"The brother of my mother has died," Thanh said dolefully, indicating the pointed stick in the path. It was taboo to entertain strangers until the family had burned the house and built another.

Death had stalked this lad's family. Long ago his father lingered too long at the alcohol jar and rolled into a nearby stream; the current swept him over a waterfall, and it was days before his battered body was found. A few months ago his sister's husband succumbed to a fever, and for many days and nights the house was filled with wailing. And now his uncle died.

This was not all. Thanh and his mother had been gravely ill, though they were recovering, and there were the usual loss of crops and the persistent cold and hunger.

Sau could understand why the youth was distraught.

"But God chooses the times of trouble to bring comfort to those who believe," he said.

"I thought God had moved away," Thanh replied. He had not waited to see if God was sufficient in distress; at the urging of others, he returned to imploring the spirits to give them a little peace.

Thanh hung his head. Having once prayed to the God of Heaven, he did not like sacrificing to the spirits now. Yet how was he to stand alone against the traditions of centuries? Ashamed to have Sau come and find him thus, he cut short the visit by running past the pointed stick and into the house.

Sau should have been downcast as he retraced his steps: not even one believer to show for all his efforts. But strangely he whistled. He had planted the Gospel seed among the Tring and Kar would be here to tend the blossoming. And while this was happening, Sau would keep going to reach the countless numbers in the mountains who still did not know God.

Sau was heartened further when he met Kar again. In his absence Kar had looked around for a spot on which to build a house. Finding one, he announced his intention to the people up and down the stream.

One man took kindly to Kar's announcement that he had come to live among the Roglai and teach them about God. His name was Ha Rong. He was a handsome fellow; his hair grew rather sparsely back from his forehead, which gave him a certain dignity usually reserved to a much older person. He stood taller than some, although it was his angular face poised on his long, thin neck that made him stand out in a crowd. Ha Rong talked well, and people listened, although they were sometimes left confused by what he said.

"My corn is the best in our tribe," he would remark somewhat boastfully, and then make his hearers wonder if he spoke the truth by adding, "My ground is stony and worthless and we'll not live through the winter."

It was the same with the look he gave people. His eyes were bright and piercing, showing candid friendship—at first. But if one gazed into them long enough, he sensed there a shiftiness that produced an uneasy feeling.

Yet Ha Rong was both intelligent and ambitious; perhaps because of these traits or because of his imposing mien and persuasive talk, he was clearly a leader. When they first met, Kar had thought that if he could win Ha Rong he would have taken a long step in winning the Tring to God.

The day after Sau returned from Thanh's house, Ha Rong went with the brothers to the site Kar had chosen for his house. Kar pointed out that the stream here was a likely place for catching fish and the slope was protected from the bitterest winds. Ha Rong agreed.

"Why don't you prove that God can make you free by building a house right next to my brother's?" Sau challenged him.

"Oh, I don't know—" Ha Rong reminded Sau that the Tring did not do this. Didn't Sau know that death awaited those who shared a single watering spot?

"Don't be afraid," Sau said. "My brother and I dip water together; see, the spirits haven't made us sick."

Ha Rong thought for some time, then he said, "I'll be willing to move here."

He left for his home before the brothers went back to theirs. He had become so eager to learn about the Spirit of the Skies that he hurried off to bring his family to this site.

But before Kar and Sau retraced their steps over the tortuous trail and down the big rock to Sixteen Peaks, Ha Rong sent word that he wanted to think it over some more.

Maybe he would come, maybe he wouldn't.

That was the way with Ha Rong. He blew first hot, then cold.

6

The Blood Covenant

THERE WAS NO LONGER any question in Kar's mind.
The time had come to leave his home in Sixteen Peaks. He was going
with his wife and children to live among the Tring. He did not un-
derestimate the difficulties that lay ahead. It would be no easy task
to win these tribespeople to the God of Heaven.

He could not burst into Tring country and frighten the people by
upsetting tradition which, in their view, meant the difference between life and death. He could only hope that in time someone—if
not Ha Rong, someone else—would come to trust him long enough
to listen to his teaching, and see that faith in God brought release
from the old anxieties.

But Kar had more immediate concerns to occupy him. Just getting
over that impossible trail from Chil country to Tring country with
his family would in itself be the hardest ordeal that he had ever
faced.

It was harder yet for Gien, who had not been up long from child-
birth. The couple had with them their four small sons. Kar carried
one boy on his shoulders and another on his back, making it necessary to swing his blanket roll around to his chest. Sometimes he carried his oldest son, too. His shoulder ax he held ready in his hand as
his only defense against any lurking tiger. Gien walked behind him
with their newborn wrapped in a blanket slung over her shoulder. A
basket containing all their belongings was strapped to her back. At
times the path dropped away so steeply that they had to crawl down
backwards. Nevertheless, they managed to make progress.

It was a little before noon of the second day on the trail when
Gien, looking up, suddenly cried out. Ahead of them was a giant rock.
It was the same one that had given Kar and Sau so much trouble.

"I can't! I can't do it!" Gien sobbed. She had used all her

strength to come this far. She doubted that she could pull her own weight up the sheer declivity. How could she make it with her baby?

Kar suggested that they sit down and rest. He, too, was discouraged, but he dared not show it. In time, his confidence returned. Taking Gien's hand in his, he smiled faintly and said reassuringly to his little wife:

"If God wants us to live among the Tring, God will get us over the rock."

Faith of such strength was not new to him. At the same time when Sau had brought him back to school after he suffered from Krong's bullying, he came to believe that God could give him the grace to bear it—and God did.

It was no different now. He squeezed her hand and said, "Let's try it."

Gien wiped her eyes with the hem of her long, black skirt. Kar wouldn't be alone in showing faith in the power of God! Fearful, but with resolve, she stood at the base of the rock and handed a son to her husband, who was about to pull himself up by means of a vine. She did not look at the sharp-edged boulders that littered the ground where she stood, but riveted her gaze on Kar, and on the frightened child clinging tightly to him. As she watched his slow climb, she prayed that the vine that held them between Heaven and earth would not give way.

Several times as they approached the top, she saw him slip and thought they would fall onto the jagged rocks. But, having come this way before, Sau knew which vine to grasp, where a foothold would afford a brief respite.

They reached the top. The ordeal for the parents, however, had hardly begun. Kar came back for the second son; this trip was just as risky. Two sons were at the top now, badly frightened and crying, but safe. What of them if anything should happen to Kar and Gien?

Kar took the blankets and the basket up on the next trip; this was easy. Then, as he mounted with the third child, Gien heard a sound that made her forget the dangers which Kar faced. Close beside her in a jungle grove a terrifying screech split the air. Hastily strapping the baby to her back, she snatched a vine trailing almost to the base of the rock and began to pull herself up. What she heard might have been the cry of a small mountain deer. Yet she

knew it could just as well be the cry of a tiger imitating a deer.
She climbed with all her might until she was well up the face of the
boulder.

Kar, who was lying flat at the top, saw how tired she was. Clutch-
ing a root with one hand, he reached down for her with the other.
Unhappily, she was just beyond his grasp. At that instant he pointed
out a place where she could rest her foot momentarily in a notch of
the granite wall; now he lowered himself to where she was able to
cling to his ankle. Starting back up, they both slipped and almost
fell. Once she bruised a knee on the rock, but by taking the blow
kept from rolling on her baby. Farther up, Kar reached down to take
her arm. Close to the top his grip was wrenched away.

"Father God! My wife is falling!"

His heart was in his throat as he saw her slip down the face of the
rock.

In her slide her hands brushed against a vine. By holding tight,
she was able to sustain herself until she could win a foothold once
more. Kar regained his grip. He pulled her to the crest. She was
barely able to walk to the clump of trees to join their wailing children.

"We're here!" Kar sighed. "We've mounted the rock!"

Both he and Gien then dropped to the ground. The trail led up
still higher and then sharply down to the lower slopes of the Tring
country. But they would make it now. Kar knew that from here on
there was no obstacle to be compared to that rock. God wanted them
to live among the Tring! There was no more question about it.

Kar and Gien wept again. Their tears were a reaction from their
ordeal, to be sure. But they were also an expression of thankfulness.

Their journey was far from the last of their hardships. When they
reached the site Kar had already picked out, he hastily built a house
for his family, a tiny one-room, barely adequate shelter. Then he
turned to the discouraging task of trying to scratch a living from the
stony, slanting sides of the mountain.

While he planted his corn, he had to hold on to bushes to keep
from falling from his field. He tried to raise pumpkin but failed.
Over the months they found the dry monsoon from overland cold and
disagreeable and the wet monsoon from the sea even colder and more
miserable.

The stream that had appeared so promising when Kar chose this
site for his home produced few fish. They felt this lack severely, for

fish was the sustaining food of a Chil family. The mosquitoes were the biggest that had ever bitten them, and they carried malaria. From the Tring, Kar and his family caught a scaly, infectious skin disease.

Yet backbreaking, futile work, and hunger, were only physical burdens. There were spiritual obstacles still to be overcome. Kar and Gien soon learned that if they were to win the people to a hearing for the Gospel, it would mean waiting perhaps for a very long time for the people to decide to grant that hearing.

Sau had every confidence that Kar would win the Tring people. He fully understood the difficulties his brother faced, but he also appreciated his qualities of enthusiasm, cheerfulness, and good humor. He would pray for Kar, and would help him when he could; to Sau it seemed only a matter of time until the Tring would be numbered among the God-Followers.

While Sau continued teaching the people of Chil villages about the Spirit of the Skies, another neighboring tribe, a mysterious and unfriendly people called the Roglai, was claiming more and more of his thought.

In his desire to reach this tribe, even Sau's most unstinting admirers thought he had met his match.

One night Sau sat at the fire of the oldest man in Sixteen Peaks.

"Doubly old father," Sau said, addressing him with respect, "if we Chil were to visit the Roglai, at what point would we try to make our first contact?"

The old man scratched his graying head. He was not quick to answer, and when he did he spoke cautiously:

"Near the banks of the Roaring River."

Then he added emphatically:

"If you are thinking of going there, put such thoughts from you. They are the people of the poisoned arrows. They would kill you."

Sau had heard that while the Tring were the most downtrodden of the mountain tribes, the Roglai were the most ferocious. They coated their arrow tips with the sap of a tree which they called the "poison tree." A bear would fall dead a hundred paces from where it was shot; an elephant a kilometer, and a man a mere step or two. Some Roglai who used it had themselves died when the poison accidentally seeped through a scratch in the skin or an open sore.

At one time, long ago, marauders from far away had raided Roglai country and carried off their children to be slaves. To make sure nothing like this ever happened again, the Roglai prepared these arrows coated with the poison. Recently, they were using them more and more against the guerrilla troops that roamed in their forests.

In former years the Roglai sometimes rode the swift current of turbulent Roaring River down to the coastal city of Nha Trang. There they worked to pay their taxes to the French and, this concession made, to buy salt. But now the fighting between the French soldiers and the jungle-based rebels of the Viet Minh made that route dangerous. The Roglai could no longer go out of their mountains. And they did not welcome others in.

When the guerrilla forces entered the Roglai country to regroup their depleted ranks or to forage for food, hardly a raiding party came out intact; and after a brush with the Roglai some parties did not come out at all. It would have been the same with the French had they gone in.

The Roglai skin was lighter than the skin of the Chil. They were the only tribe to allow their women to play the gongs. They were nearly as superstitious as the Tring. All their gods lived in the earth, so they were careful not to dig unless it was unavoidable. When they planted rice, they made only the smallest of holes in which to drop the seed.

Their sorcerers held great power. One witchdoctor known far and wide for his extraordinary influence with the demons was a slight man named La Yoan. Some sorcerers built their power on trickery; not La Yoan. By vision, by voices, by transport of his soul, he mingled with the spirit world.

Usually when he was called to the side of a sick person, La Yoan boiled a rare kind of leaf and then looked into the pot to see whether the fragments called for a pig to be sacrificed, or a chicken, or a buffalo. And with the proper sacrifice done and the deep of the night come, he would light home-molded candles and hang a string of tiny brass bells over his patient. Then closing his eyes to blot out distraction, he would joggle the bells and chant:

> Oh, Spirits, may your evil natures be appeased.
> Give health, give strength, give adequate breath;
> Become incarnate in me.

If the spirits were inclined, they invited La Yoan's soul to climb

the string to enter their mysterious domain. There in the spirit world
he met semihuman creatures. Some would be dark-skinned like the
Chil, some lighter like the Roglai. If one with a happy face appeared,
he was glad. That meant his patient would recover. Too often he
met one with downturned mouth and a menacing knife hanging at
his waist. Coming back from this encounter, La Yoan would have
bad news to report:

"The spirits will not be appeased by your sacrifice. They will not
let you regain your health."

La Yoan would rather have done anything than tell a mother her
sick child was to die or a village father that some spirit refused to
bless his corn crop. Despite the fear that made people standoffish to
La Yoan, they knew he was a kind man and gentle father. They
wished they could consider him their friend. But a sorcerer of such
power had, of necessity, to remain aloof.

For this reason, La Yoan was sad. At times he would have given
up his position. But he hadn't chosen it. The spirits had chosen him.
Neither was it his choice to step aside. There was nothing to do but
be the best servant of the demons possible.

Well, La Yoan had certainly succeeded over the years, everyone
said. When he was under the spell, he almost looked like a demon.
His eyes lost their friendliness. His youthful face grew haggard as
though clouded with age. Even his thick black hair seemed to be
galvanized by some strange, electrifying power. Stories of La Yoan's
prowess had reached Sau's ears, even though he lived as far away
as he did.

It was La Yoan, above anyone else, whom Sau wanted to meet.
He regarded him as the key to the whole Roglai tribe. Not so much
because La Yoan was a sorcerer; rather, for another reason. Two
generations ago Sau's people and La Yoan's had been joined in a
treaty of peace. That treaty was now all but forgotten and would
expire if not renewed by Sau and La Yoan.

The grandparents of La Yoan and those of Sau's wife, Drim, had
sworn peace by the pact. The quintessence of the covenant was blood
—human blood.

Years ago the Chil had dug traps for wild elephants near their
border with the Roglai. But the Roglai had burned the coverings
of the traps and the elephants escaped. This called for retaliation,

and the Chil plotted to seize ten young Roglai as slaves.

A Roglai mother proposed a compromise.

"Let us make a covenant, your village and ours," she suggested. "Instead of our children becoming your slaves, you will come to our land where the elephants roam more freely and we will trade with one another."

The Chil withdrew to their village to think it over. Safe entry into Roglai land where ivory tusks were plentiful—this prospect was tempting. But what about their revenge?

"I say make them pay," demanded a man who looked forward to getting a young slave girl.

"And when the children grow tall have them rise against us and murder us all in our beds?" countered a woman. Like the Roglai mother who suggested the compromise, she had a teen-age daughter; she could sympathize with the other woman when it came to making slaves of children.

"I say not," she declared emphatically.

Her reasoning prevailed. The Chil people of Monkey Village dispatched this mother, her husband, the couple's daughter, and the village elder to the Roglai village of Howling Water. There, around a fire under a tall teak tree, the Chil and Roglai sat down to palaver.

While the Chil girl made friends with the Roglai girl, the older ones outlined a pact of peace. The village elders exchanged bracelets. The terms would remain in force as long as each man wore the bracelet. But that was not enough. One man might be tempted to remove his metal band. Besides, the bracelet would go with him to the grave. What then? Something more was needed.

Bowls of rice alcohol were brought. First the women on one side of the fire, then the men on the other, cut their own fingers with knives and let the blood drop into the bowls. The Chil exchanged their bowls with the Roglai. While others beat a deerskin drum to call the spirits to witness, the men drank, then the women. Someone looked up to see the girls playing.

"Bring the daughters," they said.

The Chil girl's name was Duin, the Roglai girl's, Ta Hien. The two little ones took their places at the council fire.

"Let this convenant exist as long as these our daughters live," said Ta Hien's mother as the girls went through the same ritual. "And then let their children renew it."

Once the compact lapsed, war between the tribes could start at any time.

For years the people of the two villages intermingled in trading and at feasts. Duin's father, a Chil, roamed through the mountains of the Roglai until one day he came on a pleasant valley. He considered settling with his family in the valley, which was fertile and would support many people. But the heat made him sick and he had to leave.

Stopping off on his way back at Howling Water to rest and recover, he found the place deserted. He asked a man of the Roglai tribe why this was so.

"The valley is no place for people," he said in a cautious whisper. "It is a place where only the spirits dwell."

Duin's father talked of the valley, but never went back there. Gradually the people of the two villages drifted apart as the people of the convenant scattered to various places. By the time Sau was born, the trail between Monkey Village and Howling Water had disappeared.

But although there was no contact, the covenant remained. According to its terms Drim, who was Duin's daughter and direct in line, and Sau, her husband, ought to renew it. With no daughter to represent the Roglai's generation, the sorcerer La Yoan, the son of Ta Hien, would drink for the Roglai—if anyone drank.

But what chance had any Chil even to talk to the Roglai about renewal? With the Roglai sealed up to themselves and apparently liking it that way, a Chil crossing the border today would no doubt be greeted by a poisoned arrow.

Now, Sau reasoned, his people had a better covenant to offer the Roglai. It, too, was a covenant of blood. One day long ago the blood of One hanging on a Cross dropped on mankind, cleansing away the world's hurts and wrongs and leaving a joy and a peace forever renewing.

But how was Sau to offer this covenant of the Son of the God of Heaven?

He did not know—yet. There was one thing he could do now, however, to prepare for offering it someday. That was to move his people closer to the border of Roglai country so when the day came—

and he was sure it would come—they could beat a new path to Howling Water.

Oh, there were other reasons, too, for moving. The lower, warmer slopes toward the border would grow better crops of rice and corn. And though one did not talk openly about it, the Viet Minh's guerrillas had recently made exacting demands.

As Sau had foreseen that day on the trail, the guerrillas were now demanding food from the villagers. This was a serious matter, for the latter had hardly enough for themselves. Sometimes the jungle men went even further. They threatened to abduct the young men unless the youths agreed to join the Viet Minh voluntarily. The guerrillas came to see Sau. Now and then they held out tantalizing offers for him to become one of them.

One day he again met in the path a man carrying a shiny new gun.

"Our leader has won great battles in the north," the man, who wore a collarless black shirt and peasant black trousers, said to him. "The French will soon be driven from the cities of the north. Then our leader will send help to us and we will drive them from Dalat."

Sau observed that he hoped the French would soon leave the land. He felt they had been guests long enough.

"Fight with us, then, to drive them out!" the rebel urged.

"The tribesmen have no guns," Sau replied. This time he went further. He said he did not want to kill Frenchmen. He did not want to kill anyone.

Once he had risked his life to keep Frenchmen as well as Grandfather from being killed by his own. But since then much blood had flowed—the blood of Frenchmen, of the rebel soldiers of the Viet Minh, of innocent mountaineers, of promising young men and old women and tiny children in the cities of the plains. He said to the man that he wished people would not kill one another.

This rebel standing before him was a man to whom Sau felt he could talk frankly.

"There is something more," he said. "Do you say there is no God in Heaven?"

At many tribal fires he had heard it said that the guerrillas claimed there was no God. The very thought was enough to send the blood to Sau's face. Now he meant to find out if this talk were true.

"What is it that you want from your God?" asked the man in

reply. "Food? A house? Piasters to fill your pockets? Help us take these things from those who hold them now and you will have plenty."

The black-clad man, a Vietnamese, not a tribesman, spoke to Sau in French. From Sau's speech and his bright red blazer the jungle man guessed that Sau must have spent some time in Dalat.

"Have you seen the fine homes in which the Frenchmen live?" he asked.

Yes, of course, Sau had seen them. No doubt he was the better acquainted of the two with the houses of Dalat. From the man's occasional lapse into his native tongue Sau guessed he had come down from the north. Sau could tell him a few things about the houses of Dalat and about the clocks and the kettles and the other splendors to be found in the market.

"Join with us. These things will be yours, and many more," the guerrilla promised beguilingly.

Perhaps, Sau thought, this *was* a way to get the things he coveted— even the yellow house against the dark green pine trees, the one with a frangipani at its door. He didn't know. Or, rather, he did know. Of course he knew. Once he had left the man and was alone on the path, he knew that you didn't get possessions by taking them from other people. And he knew that his job was to tell people about Jesus Christ, the Son of Heaven's God. Nothing must interfere with that job.

Often he was coaxed, and his people were coaxed in various ways. But when soft words did not bring the Viet Minh the food they needed, or the men they wanted, they began helping themselves by force. When Sau told the people of Sixteen Peaks that the time had come to move, for this reason they agreed to go.

Their new village, two days' journey toward Roglai country, was built on the highest peak around. It was called Da Blah—Mountain Top. Often a cloud enveloped the site, and on clear nights frost sometimes lay on the ground. Tigers snarled in the darkness as they circled around the cluster of houses. The people cleared new fields and planted them. When the crops did not grow well, they went into the surrounding forest and discovered the wild manioc and berries to add to their diet.

Mountain Top was mostly a village of God-Followers, some one hundred fifty of them. On the highest spot they built a church, which was small and like their houses covered with tree bark. A bamboo cross crowned the gable. The pulpit had been carved from a solid tree trunk to exactly the right height for Sau.

One night as Sau was preaching from his log pulpit, he looked up to see by the light of the lantern a slim form in the doorway. It was the Tring boy, Thanh. Sau stopped preaching. Smiling past the crowd on the benches, he spoke to Thanh, telling the boy how glad he was to have him come. Thanh, however, did not smile in return. He was ragged and dirty and looked afraid. Sau walked down the aisle to him, brought him up toward the front, and told those on the first bench to squeeze together to make room for the boy.

Sau then resumed his message, directing his remarks mainly at Thanh. But the boy needed no preaching. He had felt shame for sliding back to pagan ways and his shame made him run from Sau; but later the desire to make a new beginning conquered his shame, bringing him over the mountains, the rock and all, to Sau's new village.

After the service, the boy, in tears, said, "Uncle, please ask God to take me back."

Sau prayed, and soon Thanh was praying. And the next day Thanh was as clean both physically and spiritually as Sau's own sons. Sau spent long hours in teaching the boy. One day he sent him to Dalat to continue learning from Grandfather and Grandmother.

Thanh was not the only youth to catch the vision of preaching from Sau. Doi, the Chil who had grown up among the Tring, now wanted to travel as an evangelist.

Doi had recently come to Mountain Top from helping Kar with the Tring. He often talked with Sau about the Roglai. In his unruffled way he showed enthusiasm for someday teaching the Roglai about Christ.

"I, too, want to go to them," Sau said.

If Sau could only find the way to make contact, a splendid chance to introduce the Gospel to the Roglai seemed at hand. Grandfather and Grandmother had sent word they were coming to Mountain Top for a special time of teaching.

From their earliest days in Dalat Herbert and Lydia Jackson had cared for the children of other missionaries who were sent to them for schooling. Now some new arrivals had come to take this responsibility, leaving the Jacksons free for tribal work. And with a few

G

thousand God-Followers spread through these mountains, the Christian and Missionary Alliance had sent other helpers from America.

The health of Tam, Jackson's good helper, had broken, so he was forced to leave Dalat. Before he did, however, Jackson sought others among the Vietnamese to help in the work. A couple whom the Jacksons knew well, Pham van Nam and his wife, volunteered. Coming from the Mekong Delta, they were children of well-to-do parents. However, they had turned their backs on a life of ease to labor for God among the tribespeople and became good helpers. They looked forward to the trip with the Jacksons.

The time of teaching at Mountian Top—this would be Grandfather and Grandmother's first visit—was planned for the spring of 1951. Sau got his people together to discuss it.

"They will ride small horses except where the trail is steepest," he said. "And whether they ride or walk we must make the trail safer for them."

Improvement of the trail was Sau's idea; it was an enormous task, although not beyond Sau's capacity to get the job done.

He unfolded his plans to the people; everyone fell to work with enthusiasm, eager to make travel easier for their visitors. Sau showed them where to trim back the underbrush to widen the trail, to fell trees, to build "monkey" bridges made by suspending bamboo crosspieces from strong vines, to cut into the mountainsides to make the fingernail paths more secure. And as he instructed them, he pitched in to work with them.

The time drew near for the visit. Sau thought one thing was needed to make it complete—to have La Yoan here when Grandfather and Grandmother came. What could he do? He sat by the firebox in his home one night, eating a late meal after having worked hard on the trail all day. His wife's old mother, Duin, now a stooped, gray-haired widow with long, sagging holes in the lobes of her ears, lived with the couple. As Sau ate, she was busy with her chores.

"Tell me, old mother," Sau said, looking up, "is the covenant of blood still strong enough to protect us if we travel in the Roglai country?"

For a moment she stopped her sweeping and regarded her son-in-law.

"You want to see La Yoan," she said, as if reading his thoughts. Then she added:

"Yes, you could go, since you are under the covenant."

She stopped her sweeping altogether. Standing over the iron kettle from which Sau was eating, she shook an admonitory finger.

"But who among those dealers in poison would know you are a child of the covenant? They have never seen you. Who would know you are the husband of my daughter? Who among them would know I have a daughter?"

"We know of La Yoan," Sau said. "We know he is the son of the girl whose blood you drank."

"Who does not know of La Yoan?" she shrugged. Slowly, she shook her head.

"No," she said, "you cannot go—and live to tell of it."

As though dismissing his notion, she picked up a long stick, stirred the fire, and laid an end among the coals to burn. Sau scraped the bottom of the kettle. In his heart he knew she was right.

He said no more that night. But he could not stop thinking about La Yoan and his people who lived over there in misery and fear without knowing God.

A few nights later he brought the subject up again. This time he asked Duin if, as one of those who took part in the covenant, she thought *she* could go without being killed.

"I could go—if they haven't forgotten," she said. Again she became thoughtful. "And if they recognized this gray old woman as the girl who for years after the covenant ate at their feasts."

Sau hesitated before he put his next question.

"And would you—go?"

Her heavy eyelids always drooped; now they closed altogether. He could not read her thoughts.

"Will *you* go find La Yoan and tell him that I, too, am a child of the covenant?" he asked.

It was a shocking request. Now that the words were uttered, Sau felt he must make her understand why he asked. He added:

"Will you tell him that I want him to come to our village to receive a better covenant than the old one, and to hear of a Spirit greater than all the spirits of evil he serves?"

Duin said nothing. When she did not answer, Sau began to wish

he had not brought this torment to her. He was about to say that he
had no right to expect so much, when she answered.

"I will go," she said quiely, anu taking up her broom, she began
furiously to sweep the scattered ashes.

Two days later the village took time from the elaborate preparations to bid good-by to a valiant old woman. Two young people
volunteered to go with her, a boy named Bom and a girl named
Dai. Since they were in Duin's charge, they would undoubtedly be
safe. Before Duin left, Sau prayed with her. Then he wiped away a
tear as he watched the travelers disappear into the forest.

What could an old woman and two young people do in the face of
tigers and wild pigs and snakes? And what if they got past all of these,
and the poisonous vines and torrential streams, only to find that the
Roglai failed to recognize Duin and thought rather that she had
come to spy for those they supposed were their enemies? Had the
Roglai, through loss of contact with the Chil over the years, forgotten the covenant? Or those charged with perpetuating it—might
they not have died without ever having passed on the charge? Sau
wished he could call Duin back. But she was gone.

As he returned to his work on the trail, he could not help but
wonder if he had sent the old woman to her death. Yet there was some
strange assurance in his heart. God *did* love the Roglai and wanted
them to believe.

7

Eyes with the Look of Fire

OLD, WRINKLED, AND BENT, Duin trudged along with her two young companions. The morning was cold and foggy.

Then an eerie feeling came over her. It was all strange—the thick undergrowth, the rocks, the billowing trees with their creeping vines —yet somehow all familiar. Each labored step brought a new wave of nostalgia as she recalled those days of her childhood when she had passed this way to meet those who were so unknown to her then— the Roglai.

The journey from Mountain Top to Howling Water, even with luck, would take several days. Down they would climb from peak to dark ravine and up to peak again. At one high place they would see the ocean in the distance. She remembered that they must pass near a thunderous waterfall that to her people had once been ominously sacred. Then they would start the long descent, down, down, down the sheer slopes, as the air grew steadily warmer, toward the village of Howling Water.

Armed only with a shoulder ax and walking sticks, the old woman and the young people picked their way through head-high elephant grass. Here in the swamps they stopped to fight off bloodsuckers— those slimy leeches that whipped out long, ugly feelers as the travelers drew near. On higher ground as well as in swamps, they were stung continuously by flies and mosquitoes.

One night, quite close to where they slept, they heard the anguished cry of that small animal known as a barking deer, then the trumphant yelp of a tiger. They did not sleep again that night. The next day, back on the trail, they felt the earth tremble and heard a tumultuous trumpeting. A herd of wild elephants was passing. They had to make a wide detour to keep clear of the animals' well-marked trail to a watering hole.

With every step downward, the heat grew more intense. This was another strain on the old woman, who was not used to the heavier air. The inhuman task of breaking through raw jungle taxed all her resources. Yet she kept on, and if she walked slowly, she pushed forward steadily. The faith she had learned from her son-in-law propelled her. The charge from Sau drove her on as if it had come from God.

Perhaps it had. Deep was her conviction that the poisoned-arrow people needed her ministry. She felt the weight of the commission entrusted to her.

Should the covenant die, should she die before it could be renewed, then the last hope for peace between her people and the Roglai would be gone. Yet it was not just freedom from fighting that was involved. Eternal destinies depended on her success. She had to reach the sorcerer La Yoan, the one person of his generation on his side who could bring their two tribes together.

She must not fail.

Bom and Dai should have turned back now because once in Roglai land they might be mistaken, even with their youth, for hostile outsiders. Yet they did not complain, but with the aged Duin forged ahead. On the fifth day they arrived at the narrow, swift stream known as Roaring River.

Duin sighed with relief. Now she knew where she was going.

"We travel downstream, maybe for half a day," she said, and her voice rang with new confidence.

They were really in Roglai territory at last. She did not need to caution her comrades. Wherever they could, they kept to the shadows of the trees. Finally, they came on an area of thick bamboo and large rocks.

From these rocks and the noise of the river Duin recognized the place where once had stood the village of the blood covenant. From their concealment near the river she recognized even the very spot of enactment.

"See, there up the hill is the ancient teak under which we drank the blood alcohol!" she whispered to the others.

Among the boulders near the old tree, near a path to the river, stood three houses. The roofs sagged so that at first Duin thought they were abandoned. She could not understand this, for the path was freshly trodden. Just then, from one of these huts came the sound of loud argument. Suddenly a dozen people poured out.

They were a thin and hungry-looking lot, clad only in loincloths or skirts of bark. They jostled one another rudely. This pushing, poking, shouting vortex of quarrelers moved slowly in the direction of the river, sorting themselves as they squabbled into two groups knotted around two apparent adversaries. One seemed to be the accuser, the other the accused, in some bitter incomprehensible dispute.

"They're coming to the river for a water judgment," Duin called softly to Bom and Dai. She knew these tribal rituals well: the quarrel could go on all day before the judgment ended it. And then most likely they would follow it up with protracted sacrificial rites. She decided this was the moment to show herself.

"I will go alone," the old woman said, turning to the young people. "If the Roglai receive me, it will be safe for you to come out. If they put a poisoned arrow in me, do not try to help me. Go back by the way we came."

She threw a dead branch into the path, quite near the crowd. Immediately the clamor stopped. For a brief moment the Roglai stood motionless, frozen in terror, like a figures in some strange tableau. Then instinctively they fled into cover, vanishing almost magically. Duin emerged; she had the path to herself. Now, from concealment, it was they who eyed her.

Groping for the words of their tongue that once she had known so well, she called out:

"I, this old mother of the Chil . . . greet you . . . peace . . . peace!"

Her daring in stepping forth nearly overwhelmed her. How foolish she was! She knew they would be suspicious; a grayed old woman bursting upon them could only be one to lure them into the sights of bowmen still hidden among the trees. Of course they would think that —unless they recognized her as a daughter of the covenant.

Clinging to the hope that someone would recognize her, she stepped falteringly up the path, turning her face to the right and to the left.

"Ta Hien . . . my sister . . . do you know me? You drank my blood for peace!" she cried. But her voice quavered with age and fright. Words eluded her. She continued speaking in Chil. But, she wondered, would anyone understand her?

Peace—she had called out the word they used on that day so long ago. Would any among these edgy warriors know it now? As she waited for response, any response, she remembered how she and Ta Hien had run up and down this path and hid among the rocks. What wonderful fun they'd had that day while the older ones sat over their alcohol jars and talked, sometimes sulkingly, about the terms of peace.

Was Ta Hien alive today? Duin had not been able to pick her out in the melee, but that meant little, for her drooping eyelids did not permit her to see too well.

"Ta Hien!" she called once more.

A woman stepped from a thicket onto the path. She was gray like Duin, but taller and more erect. She walked slowly forward, and the smile of recognition came to her face.

"It is you, Duin . . . it is you," Ta Hien said softly again and again. "A daughter of the Chil with whom my people once made peace."

The two old sisters of the pact now stood in the path together; they grasped each other by the arms in the greeting of friendship. Smiling, Duin looked up at Ta Hien; at the same time, she cast a thankful glance toward Heaven.

There was a difference in their languages, but what were words, or years or changing circumstances, to a friendship that still endured.

Ta Hien took her visitor by the arm and led her up the path toward the settlement. She called assurances to her people; one by one they left their hiding places and came out, anxious for a look at the stranger.

Duin signaled to Bom and Dai, who also came out. Soon they were all at the houses; the village quarrel was overshadowed and forgotten for the moment by an event of greater interest.

In a mixture of languages and signs they shot questions and answers back and forth. One or another of the Roglai remembered this certain Chil or that and asked particularly about him.

Did the old Chil sorcerer still live? No; he died, and no one had taken his place. Had tigers eaten many people in recent days? None at all; Heaven had protected them. Who owned the most buffalo? As a matter of fact, only a few pigs remained, and some of them would soon be slain to feed visitors who were coming. Were the Chil friends or enemies of the Roglai?

This brought Duin to the point of her mission.

"You, Ta Hien, are the mother of the sorcerer, La Yoan," she said. Ta Hien was pleased that her son's fame had spread so far.

"You know of him?" she asked eagerly.

"The husband of my daughter has sent me in search of him," Duin replied.

Her remark had a strange effect on the gathering. No one wanted to say anything more. Ta Hien looked away and others found things to occupy their attention. One old man finally broke the silence.

"His home is the forest," he said. "He was fearful that the jungle men would come some night and spear him while he slept."

"That's why he left his house," explained another. He pointed out an abandoned hut as the place where La Yoan once had lived.

"They are angry at him. He refused to give them corn when they asked," said still another.

They talked freely once more. Someone said that La Yoan feared the French more than the jungle men. Another spoke of how faithfully he used to ride the river down to the coastal city to pay his tax, but now that the Viet Minh was encamped around Nha Trang he could no longer go there.

"Because he has not paid, he fears that a man of his position would suffer if caught by the French," Ta Hien added.

"I would like to see La Yoan," said Duin.

Again they fell quiet. The sorcerer's mother broke the silence this time.

"That is not easy," she said. "We dare not reveal where he lives."

Duin looked crestfallen. Had she come so far only to be unable to fulfill her mission? She forced back her eyelids to gaze squarely at Ta Hien in an effort to convey her disappointment. Evidently she was successful, for Ta Hien spoke. Because Duin was of the covenant, she said, the Roglai must consider her as friend.

"He has a field in which he grows his sugar cane and rice. I will show you how to reach it. Go there and you can meet him. But the young ones must stay here."

The talk now rested mainly with the two old women. Believing Duin sought out La Yoan to beg him to entreat the spirits, the Roglai forgot her and took up the quarrel where they had dropped it.

"I say you led the jungle men to my storehouse," the accuser said to his adversary. He was speaking of a raid by the Viet Minh guer-

rillas the night before, Vehemently, the accused denied it. Some
supported one, some the other, and off toward the river they went
again to judge the truth by water.

This was not the kind of judgment that Sau would have tolerated,
Duin said to herself as she watched them go. She had seen him call
both sides to present their arguments and afterward decide between
them. In a water judgment, the spirits decided. The contenders
submerged themselves in a stream. The one unlucky enough to come
up for air first was the loser; by this sign the villagers knew that his
breath had been cut short by offended spirits. Thus proven wrong, he
would be punished, perhaps even killed by members of his own
household. The winner, on the other hand, did not always put in an
appearance to claim his damages.

From where she sat in front of the houses Duin saw the head of
the accuser come up first. As punishment for being wrong he would
have to pay three pigs to the man he unjustly charged. But the innocent man would never be able to collect. He had stayed under the
water so long that he drowned. Not until the next day, however, was
his body found, caught on an overhanging branch downstream.

Three days after the water judgment Ta Hien, giving in to Duin's
urging that she be taken to La Yoan's field, persuaded a young
Roglai to guide her. The tribesman finally led her to a sloping patch
of sugar cane and mountain rice. He refused to stay, however, saying
that La Yoan would be furious that he had brought her.

"You will know him—he's short, and when he communes with the
spirits he has the look of fire in his eyes," he said, and promptly
disappeared. There was nothing for Duin to do but sit on the ground
and wait.

She drowsed. She awoke in the late afternoon to find La Yoan
standing over her.

"You seek me?" He spoke in the tongue of the Vietnamese, which
Duin understood better than the dialect of the Roglai.

She got to her feet and turned her half-closed eyes up to look
at him. He was shorter than she had thought he would be. Why, he
was no taller than she. He appeared strong, though; his naked chest
and arms were muscular. He had a wide, flat nose and his young
face seemed to bespeak friendliness. His eyes were quite sunken, but
she saw no flame of spiteful fire in them. She could not picture this
man as one who consorted with demons.

He smiled. Perhaps, she thought, he would not be so hard to handle after all.

"My mother sent me word. She says that you drank the covenant with her many years ago," he recalled rather gently.

Duin agreed that this was so.

"I am a child of the covenant," he continued. "You and your children are of the covenant, too. You are welcome."

He pointed out that they could talk after they reached his home, and beckoned her to follow him. He turned into a scarcely visible path, and they walked until the sunlight no longer filtered through the trees. In the growing dusk Duin could hardly keep on the trail; she was glad when he stopped and indicated they had arrived.

But what was this! Had she not been here before?

There ahead were the rocks that marked the site of the Village of Howling Water. And the noise of the river came from below them. Somewhere around was the giant old teak and the clearing with its three sagging houses. Why had he brought her back full circle instead of taking her to his hidden home in the forest?

La Yoan stood in the path, listening and looking. After a while he whistled quietly. Then he led Duin around a clump of bamboo and behind a huge boulder.

There, in a sheltered space, the warm glow of a fire greeted her. The scene was homelike. A woman sat at the fire tending her cooking pots. Several children, quite naked, played nearby.

La Yoan nodded a greeting to the woman, but offered no word of explanation as to why he brought home a guest. Perhaps she expected the visit, just as La Yoan had known that Duin sought him. The little man dropped to a mat next to the fire; he signaled to Duin to do likewise.

For the first time she noticed that this forest home was located at the mouth of a cave. How naturally the big rock hid the opening and the fire! One walking the obscure trail would never guess that so close at hand lived a family with their chickens, pigs, and goats.

As she looked around, Duin could now make out small mounds inside the cave. These would be the family's modest food supply— heaps of manioc and unflailed rice. From a peg driven into a crevice hung a crossbow and quiver of arrows and a string of tiny brass bells.

"We will eat while you talk," La Yoan said to Duin, placing a bowl of rice and jungle leaves in her hands. But La Yoan did the talking, leaving Duin to listen and to eat and to steal glances at the wondering children.

He spoke first of his fields and the depredations of both rats and elephants. Then he shifted the conversation. There was a touch of suspicion in his voice. "You say you are Duin, the girl of the Chil who before my birth drank my mother's blood."

"I am the one," Duin assured him.

"Why do you seek me?"

"I come bearing a message from Sau, my daughter's husband. You have heard of Sau?"

"We Roglai find it hard to understand your tongue," La Yoan replied. "And when we do, we have little interest in what takes place outside our forest . . . No, I do not know your daughter's husband."

"He is a believer," she explained. "And, like you, he is the one, with his wife, my daughter, to renew the pact of friendship between us."

"We have observed no covenant during my lifetime," said La Yoan indifferently.

"But we have in mine," retorted Duin. "Do you believe the span of your years to be more important than mine?"

"No, old mother," he said, bowing his head in deference to her age. "Do you come to ask me to meet your son-in-law?"

"I do," she replied. She was relieved; at least he understood her mission. "But he sends word that he wishes to show you a better covenant than one accomplished by human blood in rice alcohol."

La Yoan exhibited mild surprise.

"What could be stronger?" the little sorcerer asked. He thought he knew all there was to know about potions and elixirs.

"The blood of the Son of Heaven's God, whom we in our village worship."

La Yoan said nothing. In silence, he refilled their bowls. Before taking another mouthful, Duin observed that they ought to thank God for the food. This seemed to puzzle La Yoan.

"But this rice came from my field on the slopes of the mountain, and the leaves my wife gathered herself," he protested. "Why do you say we should thank another?"

"You will understand, young son of the forest," Duin replied patiently, "when my son-in-law explains God's goodness to you."

That night as the wife kept wood on the fire and the children slept at its edge, Duin recounted for La Yoan the story of the covenant. The sorcerer said that he had heard it from his mother, but he was too busy entreating the evil spirits on behalf of his people to give it much thought.

"I consort with the spirits often," he observed to his guest. "Yet mine is a calling that wearies me. I am also frightened by it." He stared moodily into the fire.

"You see, if I made a mistake in choosing the proper sacrifice, it may not only bring death to the one who lies sick before me, but in their wrath the spirits may choose to kill me too."

He paused.

"Old woman," he sighed, shaking his head, "it is not a life to seek." La Yoan went on to describe the dilemma of one who tried to please both the demons and man. But since he was careful to shut out no new spirit from his experience, when Duin finally got in a word about the Spirit of the Skies, he grew silent and listened with great interest.

"All I know are earth gods," he said later that night. "Tell me more about the One above, and also about the remarkable Son, old mother."

The fire ate much wood while Duin told how she and her people had escaped a life of hopelessness—how they now sang at their work and entrusted their sick into the hands of the God who loved them. But again and again she said that Sau should be the one to teach him.

"This is something to know," La Yoan said at last. "I would like to have the husband of your daughter teach me more."

Duin leaned forward. She put her hand on the sorcerer's arm. She sensed that at last her mission was on the threshold of success.

"Sau wishes you to come to our village."

La Yoan looked at her curiously, but said nothing.

"He would like you to come back with me for a very special reason."

"What reason?" asked La Yoan.

"Some people are coming soon to teach us all. They can teach you at the same time."

"Who are these people?"

"I only know they mean a great deal to Sau. They are from Dalất —a white man and his wife."

"A white man!" La Yoan's face grew taut. Now she saw those eyes of fire. He leaped to his feet, kicking a log so that it showered sparks. Instinctively, his fingers closed around the handle of the knife at his waist.

"Old woman, I should have known it from the first. You are a spy for the white man!" he shouted. "You have been told that for a long time I have not left these mountains to pay my tax. Neither have my people. And now the Frenchman has sent you to find me so he can speed his soldiers to my hiding place." His voice dropped. "Well, it will not be so easy. We have our arrows and our poison."

"No, no!" protested Duin. She felt him standing over her, breathing on her. She knew that she, an old woman, could die quickly under his hand. Still, Sau had said she was to bring him back, and her unfinished task gave her courage.

"The white man I spoke of is not French; he is American." Nothing came to her tongue except words that had little meaning even for her.

La Yoan shrugged.

"American? I do not know what American is." He seemed in no mood to listen to an explanation if, indeed, she could give one.

"They do not want your money or your goods or your labor," she said, desperately trying to reassure him.

But La Yoan was deeply in debt to a colonial government. He hardly found this possible to believe.

"Why not?" he demanded.

She thought for a moment, then spoke the only thought that came to her:

"They come to give—not to get."

La Yoan entered the cave and soon came out wrapping himself in a blanket.

"I do not know if what you say is a lie or true," he said, and he found a place among his sleeping children to settle down. "By morning I will make up my mind."

Soon he slept; looking at him, Duin knew that in the troubled mind of this imaginative, mercurial servant of the spirits rested not only her fate, but that of her family and friends in Mountain Top —of all her people—and the fate of the Roglai as well.

"Go to sleep, old mother," La Yoan's wife said quietly, getting up to stir the fire. "Usually he is not an unreasonable man."

8

A Valley and Unreachable Heights

THE VILLAGE OF MOUNTAIN TOP made ready for the visit of Grandfather and Grandmother. While Sau directed the preparations a feeling of great warmth flooded over him as he thought of what the two missionaries had done for his people.

It had not been many years since he himself had sat with his fellow villagers around the glazed green jars, sucking out the potent liquor. The villagers spent their days waiting fearfully for the demons' —or nature's—next move against them. Quite often for weeks at a time they simply sat; there was nothing else to do. Oh, some things needed looking after. But what incentive was there to harvest, for example, when the sorcerer, by command of the spirits, most likely would order the crop destroyed?

The drinking bouts and sacrificial feasts were the only events to which they could look forward with any anticipation.

That was how it had been for years—an unbroken cycle of fear, apathy, and drunken orgy followed by fear, apathy, and another orgy.

Then Grandfather and Grandmother had come to Dalat. Gathering young tribesmen about them, the missionaries opened their eyes to the possibility that life could hold something more. And when the young men—and some young women, too—went back to their villages with this new knowledge planted deep within them, great changes began to erupt in the mountains.

"I found people transformed," a professor of the French Lycée in Dalat observed with wonder, after making a trip to a mountain village with the missionary one day. What the government had not been able—or willing—to do for the neglected tribesfolk, the Gospel of Christ accomplished. Not all of them changed by any means. A growing number, however, were finding happiness in being free from enslavement to the spirits, in communion with their families, in working their fields to get a crop, rather than in the alcohol jar.

The habits of tribal settlements began to change as men and
women stood firm in their belief in God, and because of their stand,
were joined by others.

But those who dared to be first to forsake the jar and sacrifices
often suffered for their boldness.

In one settlement a man was chained up in a tiny pigsty because
he broke village solidarity by becoming a God-Follower. The pen
was hardly big enough for him to turn around in; he could only sit
bent over, since the sty was roofed to keep out prowling tigers. The
filth was indescribable.

"You will stay there until you join us in calling on the spirits," the
village elder said. "Our people are angry that you have undermined
the power of our sacrifices."

The man did not recant. In time he was released and others asked
him to teach them about the power of this God who had sustained
him. The band grew. Soon the whole community turned away from
demon worship to serve the One Eternal Spirit.

The sorcerers complained they were finding no work to do. Now
that people prayed, they no longer sought the witchdoctor's mystical
cure.

"Why is it people no longer come to me?" one old sorceress
lamented. "It used to be that a man got sick and I would say, 'A
pig for the pain in your back,' or 'A chicken, uncle, if you want to
lose the ache in your head.'"

Once she informed an old ailing man that he had leprosy. *That*
was a clever stroke. He was a man rich in buffalo and gongs and jars.

"The price of invoking the spirits for you?" she said, repeating
his question one day. "Just bring me a set of old and valuable gongs."

And when she had wrested away his wealth she pronounced the
man cured. How her fame spread after that! And her wealth increased.

But one day Sau came to her village. In his basket he carried
bottles of pills and tins of ointments. The people seemed to prefer
his treatments—and not only his medicines but his God, too.

A number of sorcerers turned to God. Of all converts these seemed
the most steadfast in their faith. The ones who had lived by deceit
knew the hollowness of their deception; the pagans who had been
dependent on their contact with the spirit world were relieved to be
free of it.

As God-Followers, the people worked diligently in tending their fields, and their families were better fed for it. No longer were they required to throw away corn or rice because a spirit disapproved.

If a man had laid some by, they were able to barter now and then for the clothing they needed for warmth.

A man could hold up his head. A whole village could laugh without the laughter being a cover-up for an anxiety that for spirit worshipers never faded.

The God-Followers loved music. K'Sol had translated hymns into their language and Sau was the first to play these on their instruments. They used the gourd pipes and strings and the rolling, rhythmic brass gongs to express their joy. They sang at their work, on the trail, in their fields, everywhere. A puzzled old pagan once asked:

"Won't the spirits be angry if they find you happy so much of the time?"

Most of the God-Followers enjoyed the times when they gathered in the church. To call people to service, two men beat on the big village drum; it still bore the bloodstains of sacrifices of years ago, but like the gongs, it was now played for God. The people lost no time in assembling. And why not? How close they sensed God was! God spoke to them through their Scriptures. They talked to God in prayer.

In the church was a warmth, an inexplicable glow. Partly from this frequent gathering, partly from the peace they felt toward each other, the God-Followers were knit together as no other people.

Yes, Sau thought in retrospect, Grandfather and Grandmother had done much for them.

With the visit of the missionaries at hand, several days of satisfying fellowship stretched before them. Sau's first move on the day Grandfather and Grandmother were to arrive, was to inspect the village church. He wanted to make sure there were enough ferns and pine boughs and crisp yellow-and-white mountain flowers to garnish it well. He knew that this would be the greatest day his people had ever experienced. It was their first chance to express appreciation to the ones who had brought them joy. He wanted nothing to go amiss.

When Sau had first heard that Grandfather and Grandmother were coming, a number of villagers asked him what they could do for their guests. They had only simple things for gifts. Sau reminded them they had their skills and nature's bounty.

"Let's work to make everything beautiful," he said.

The whole village was now decorated. A church doorway in Dalat had inspired Sau with the idea for a giant archway to stand in front of the church. The men had made it from slender tree trunks, twined it with evergreen, and topped it with a bamboo cross. Between the archway and the church they erected an arbor of vines and large ferns. Within this half-wall they set two seats carved from logs, as well as several benches from the church. In front of the seats they stretched a straw mat; on the mat a wild orchid sprouted from a gourd.

Sau stepped out of the church and into this arbor. A man rushed up, stretched wide his fingers, and asked, "Will a three-hand pig be enough to feed our guests today?"

"Kill two pigs," Sau advised. He hurried down to the newly built wash house below the village to check on bamboo piping that brought water from a cold mountain stream. Just as he suspected, one section leaked. He told the builders to put in a new piece. How could they expect their guests to bathe in a place with a muddy floor?

Climbing back to the clearing at the crest of the mountain, he looked at the sun. The moment had come to send the welcoming parties to their posts. Quickly, the word spread through the long-houses. The villagers crowded around Sau to hear his instructions.

"Six gongers and the men with the drum will go first," he said. He indicated the direction from which the visitors would come. "You will proceed halfway to the next village and stop there. When our guests draw near you, begin to play. As they come, join in behind."

The advance party moved out briskly. Next went a chorus of girls, each wearing a white blouse and carrying a long palm leaf. They were to hide outside a fern-covered arbor a half-hour's walk down the trail. Then, as the column passed through the arbor, they would burst into song and wave their palms. Sau sent the older men next. Moving out to their station just beyond the valley below the clearing, they rehearsed the French and Vietnamese greetings in which Sau had drilled them.

A second group of gong players gathered at the village entrance. A third took places in front of the church. Sau went back to the chapel; standing at the door, he looked at the archway and the arbor and smiled. He approved of all that had been done.

Yet in the swirl of preparation Sau was troubled. He was haunted by thoughts of Duin. There had been no word from his old mother-in-law. Would she bring back La Yoan? Would she return without him? Would she and her young companions come back at all?

He knew if they did not, he would be filled with remorse. He would blame himself.

He thought of La Yoan and of the Roglai. Would they ever know the joy that his people knew? His brother Kar had come all the way from Tring country with some of his friends especially to meet Grandfather and Grandmother. A few among the Tring had begun to trade their fear for faith, just as Sau knew they would under Kar's teaching. If the Tring, why not the Roglai? he asked. Someday they would, if only he could reach them with the Gospel!

And this he was confident he could do, if only La Yoan would come.

Turning to the work at hand, Sau sent the women back to their tasks of cleaning up the children and the houses and of cooking. He visited a storehouse to check on the supply of squash and sweet potatoes that he would present to the missionaries at the end of their visit. He went back to the church where young Doi was rehearsing a choir of boys.

"Sing loud," Sau called, flashing them an approving grin. He left the church to find that two of his scouts had arrived.

"They're on their way," one of the youths said breathlessly. Sau noticed one of the runners wore a bracelet. He said he would like to have it as a present for the guests.

That gave Sau an idea.

"Go into the houses and gather more bracelets—and beads from the women, too," he said. "We are having many guests."

He himself went home, put on a bright flowered tie that Grandfather had once given him, slipped on the coat to his suit, and fastened a large, heart-shaped pin to his lapel. Now he was ready to receive his visitors.

They were in sight at last, and when finally the long, single line of missionaries, student preachers, carriers, and neighboring tribesmen had entered the village, the population of Mountain Top was nearly doubled. The arbor overflowed. The time for speeches and presents was here.

Herbert and Lydia Jackson sat in the honor seats in the arbor.

"They gave us water and wood when we slept on their land," said Sau. "Now we have small gifts for them."

From Drim he took a pan of uncooked rice and two fresh eggs, representing the basis of a daily diet, and gave them to the missionaries.

"Grandfather and Grandmother will know a tiny bit by our gifts how much we love them," he said, smiling broadly.

Others of Mountain Top also presented the guests with rice and eggs, long, fat, green jungle bananas, chicken, beads, and bracelets. Then over cracked cups of hot green tea, ceremony dissolved in the comfortable hum of informal talk. Downing cup after cup, Sau spoke with each of the newcomers, shifting adeptly from his native tongue to French or Vietnamese or to another tribal dialect in trying to make each one feel at ease.

Today he lived a dream. Grandfather and Grandmother were actually here in Mountain Top!

Sau was one who could anticipate needs, so he decided to take a spare clay firebox to his house to see that his guests were kept warm during the night.

He was mounting the notched pole to his veranda when through a clump of bushes he saw a strange little man staring at him.

Sau thought he must be a basket carrier from Dalat and continued up the pole. Then he hesitated. If the man were a basket carrier, he would have been fully clothed. But this one wore only a loincloth. Sau had also noticed a look of fright in the deep-sunken eyes.

He set the firebox on the veranda. As he started back down the pole, he caught sight of a woman carrying a heaping basket of rice into the house where the cooking was going on. She looked like his mother-in-law.

It was! Duin was back! Wasn't that like her, to return from her arduous journey, and seeing there was work to be done, to pitch right in without a word. How relieved he was at the sight of her. He hurried toward her, eager to hear of her trip, to learn if the covenant was still in force—when suddenly he remembered the frightened man in the brush.

La Yoan! It must be the sorcerer! Duin had completed her mission fully and brought him back with her from the village of the Roglai. Sau raced from his house out to the thicket of underbrush. He pulled up short. There he found not one frightened man, but three. Sau smiled his kindliest, and slowly advanced toward them.

"I am Sau," he said, speaking first in his own tongue, then in French, and finally in Vietnamese, hoping to be understood in one of them. "And you . . ." he hesitated, ". . . and you are La Yoan?"

The stocky little man stared, then lowered his head and said, "I am La Yoan."

It was the tongue of the Vietnamese which La Yoan understood. Sau spoke in it to reassure the men. In this place of seclusion he squatted to speak further with them. La Yoan talked only with reluctance; but in answer to Sau's questions he said his friends had come over with him from Howling Water at Duin's invitation.

It was plain, however, that all three were wishing that they had not come.

Sau asked La Yoan why he was afraid.

The little man pointed to the tall impressive archway decorated with pine garlands. "That—for one thing," he said.

And the cross on top—was it a sacrificial mast? What did they intend to do—try to attract the most powerful of spirits? Were they about to call on gods he did not know and with whom he had not the slightest influence?

He was afraid, too, because so many people were here. La Yoan had never seen such a crowd in a mountain village.

Most of all La Yoan was frightened of the white people around whom everyone congregated.

Sau tried to calm his fears by giving him direct answers to his questions. Then he said to La Yoan:

"I have heard that you are a powerful sorcerer."

"I have my connections with the spirits," said La Yoan in a matter-of-fact voice.

"Don't they keep you from being afraid?" asked Sau, knowing they did not, but nevertheless wanting to hear the confession from the sorcerer's own lips.

"The people I see here are happy people," La Yoan replied, "and against happy people even my greatest charms fail."

He would have run back home if he had known the way. Then Duin brought a roasted chicken to the secluded circle. The Roglai refused it. Because of their fear, they had no appetite.

"You are a child of the covenant," La Yoan said to Sau. "I do not fear you. But the others I do fear. Yet"—his face wrinkled in bewilderment as he looked around him—"I see the people here as good ones."

That evening Sau coaxed La Yoan from his hiding place and took the sorcerer with him to the service. Together they sat on the front bench in the church. Whatever words La Yoan couldn't understand, Sau translated in a hoarse whisper in the sorcerer's ear. Yet it wasn't the words that seemed so hard for the little man to grasp; rather, it was their message.

One villager in the front of the church stood up and told how once long ago he had met a tiger in the path. "It stood between me and my house," he related. "The tiger went away, but not until he had made me fear for my life. I don't want sin to come between me and God that way," he concluded.

La Yoan could understand about a tiger, he whispered to Sau, but what was this sin the man talked about?

The meeting ended. The people lit their torches and made their way through the black night from the church to their homes. After seeing to the comfort of his guests from Dalat, Sau led the three Roglai men to one of the houses for the night.

Then, sleepless himself, he returned to the big archway. He stood and watched the fires in the houses grow dim one by one. Then he sat down in one of the carved chairs in the arbor, but in a moment was up and pacing, cracking his knuckles and kicking at stones that showed up in the first light of the rising moon.

He was sleepless tonight because his heart was burdened.

Pacing, thinking, praying, he tried to sort out the things that troubled him. But why should he be troubled at all? Hadn't Grandmother exclaimed over Sau's village, Sau's pulpit, even over the comforts in Sau's house? There was no house in the mountains to match his, Sau said to himself rather proudly. No village had ever given visitors so cordial a welcome.

Grandmother's praise still rang in his ears.

"Dear Sau, you've made it all so beautiful," she had said.

Yes, everything had come off well. *Why was he not happy? What was missing?*

Sau remembered that he'd had no time to talk with Grandfather about his plans for reaching others with the Gospel. He recalled that during the weeks he and his people had worked on the trail and prepared the village for the visit, his preaching suffered.

Could it be this that irked his soul?

Why was his mind so easily drawn to wondering if Grandfather and Grandmother liked the new hardwood bed he had made and the mosquito net he had bought in Dalat? Why was it so hard to think of what God might do for them during this time of special teaching?

Were his house and his field and all these piasters piling up in a rice bowl a part of his problem?

He saw it as good for God's people to hold high their heads. Did not abundance impress the tribesmen who measured life by the things that they had—or hoped to have someday? The temptation was strong, almost overpowering, for him to cut down his ministering to tend bigger fields just to prove this point.

Temptation came not only from within, but also from without.

The jungle men he met on the trails often held out glowing promises of wealth and power if he would join their fight to make the Viet Minh prevail throughout the land.

Temptation was severe, yet he did not give way. Not yet. He fought off the urge to enlarge his field at the expense of teaching his people about God. And as for the Viet Minh—he gave in to neither promises nor demands.

How long, he wondered, could one hold out? If a man thought he was in need of certain things and ways to get them came along, might he not be tempted past the breaking point?

It bothered Sau that this was an issue he had never quite resolved.

The jungle men created another problem. His people had moved once, partly to escape their harshness. How sad, he thought, if they should have to move again!

He wanted to do the will of God. The wife of Nam, the Vietnamese missionary who had come with Grandfather and Grandmother, had spoken that evening in the church. She had plainly said to put God first! He had prayed then, and here in the arbor tonight he prayed, "God first, Sau last."

Sau knew that above all else God wanted him to win the unhappy pagans around him. He was concerned that something might interfere. He wanted those without hope—the fear-ridden pagans—to be the burden of burdens upon him. He recalled that three of these hopeless ones were in his village right now. So he walked quietly through

the archway and down the knoll on which the church stood and to
the longhouse where he had left La Yoan.

He found the little man huddled in a dim corner. Strange. The
power of this man's witchcraft was great. His reputation reached
beyond many mountain ranges. Yet here, away from home, he was
cowering, afraid. Had he, like K'Sol, come up against a power greater
than his evil spirits? K'Sol, too, had possessed great power through
a ruthless ability to control the lives of men. But once he had encountered the power of God, he was never the same again.

Sau stepped over many sleeping bodies. La Yoan was awake.
Sau sat down beside him; until far into the night he tried hard to
make the sorcerer understand about God.

The next evening as they both sat on the front bench again to hear
the teaching of the missionaries, La Yoan confided to Sau that the
God he saw these people serving must be the true God. He asked Sau
and Nam to pray with him. He knew now what sin was; he'd always
known—only he called it by another name. He prayed for God to
forgive him for sinning and to cleanse him.

Over dying embers in many of the houses the next night people
talked of La Yoan's prayer. Had a Roglai—a sorcerer at that—truly
received the God of Heaven? Or had he spoken words because Sau
persuaded him to do so?

In the days of the gathering that remained La Yoan lost his fear.
He even entered into the games Kar directed—the wrestling that
proved the strength of lithe brown bodies; the races; the rope-jump-
ing; the pushing by two sides of a long, skinned pole until it bent in
the middle and snapped. This dour Roglai was always smiling now.
He shook the hand of the missionaries, convinced that they had come
to help him, not to do him harm.

"I will go back to my land and tell my people that they are good,
and that God is good, and that the Chil want to be our friends," he
said to Sau on the final morning of his visit.

He left on the same day that the people of Mountain Top tearfully
bade good-by to their guests from Dalat. Duin went back with him
to Howling Water to tell him again about God.

Sau arranged his affairs so he could make more frequent trips to
La Yoan's land. He found La Yoan's simple faith to be real. Those

who had doubted him were wrong. La Yoan had thrown away the rare leaves and the string of brass bells of his sorcery. Sau found he had even burned a handful of rice in a field, always before considered a taboo, to prove that the Spirit of the Skies was true and the evil spirits of earth were powerless to curse him for the impudent act of disobedience.

But there had been testing.

Once La Yoan's neck had swelled into a ball.

"It is his just compensation for forsaking the spirits," a woman said one day to Ta Hien. His mother said nothing. What could she say? In spite of his affliction La Yoan kept on singing happy songs about the God of Heaven.

On one visit Sau learned that some of the Roglai had been so disturbed by the change in the little sorcerer that they plotted to kill him.

"I heard them talking, but was not afraid," said this one who once had been so fearful of being speared while he slept. "I asked God to take care of me." La Yoan had never been unkind to his people as a servant of the demons, and now that he lived for God, there was nothing he would not do to help them.

Who could carry out threats against so accommodating a man? No one. His fellow tribesmen found in him a friend.

On one of Sau's trips, La Yoan met him with an urgent request. "Please send us a teacher who will live among us." Sau had just the man—young Doi, who kept at him about going to the Roglai.

Doi spoke only when he had something to say. One of those times came shortly after he married Dai, the young girl who had traveled with Duin and Bom to make the first contact with La Yoan. Doi said to Dai that he was going to teach the Roglai; he wanted her to come, though he knew tradition demanded that she live under her mother's roof. Dai tried to dissuade her husband from going, but his mind was made up.

"I will go tomorrow morning," he said firmly.

He loved his new wife, and he knew it would be hard for her to break their custom, but he heard God's call so strongly that he dared not turn a deaf ear.

Early the next morning he asked his wife once more if she would go, but Dai said no.

"Good-by," he said sadly. "I will come back as often as I can."
He strapped on his basket and set off on the path to Howling Water.

He had not gone far when he heard hurried footsteps behind him.
Turning, he faced Dai. She was coming, determined that God had
called her, too. As she said good-by to her mother, she had shouted
over her shoulder:

"I will come back as often as I can."

It was of such stuff that the teachers of the Roglai were made.
Between Doi's teaching and La Yoan's witness, those Roglai who
lived within a day's travel of Howling Water were deeply changed. A
year after La Yoan's conversion, the Jacksons returned to Mountain
Top; this time Doi and La Yoan brought twenty-nine Roglai who
had become believers to meet them.

Deeper and deeper, Sau roamed in Roglai territory, seeking out
those who had not heard about God. This was dangerous. He might
stumble into a nest of jungle men who would mistake him for a
hostile Roglai. Also, for every peaceful village there were a hundred
that thought strangers should be kept away by poisoned arrows.

On one trip he took a dozen Chil from Mountain Top and two
Roglai men to a large pagan village, leading the men nearly a day's
journey beyond Howling Water. Mainly they followed the Roaring
River until waterfalls in the steepening mountains made that way too
rough. Then he chose to go up and over a high peak. As they reached
a rocky crest, they looked back the way they had come and saw the
mountains of Roglai and Chil country.

Turning around, they were confronted by a great open plain.

Mountains walled in the valley on three sides; the fourth side
stretched away toward the sea. It wasn't a true plain, for undulating
hills marked it; tropical forest covered the land, and this wide green
mat was cut only by the river that flowed out of the mountains and
to the ocean.

The river wasn't so wide that a man couldn't throw a stone across
it. Yet dividing the valley as it did, the blue ribbon dominated the
scene. It was a highway, albeit with its many rapids a rough one.
This was the river over which the Roglai had traveled to the coast
in former days to pay their taxes and trade for salt.

As they drank in the breath-taking panorama, no one spoke. But
each man had his thoughts. Sau had seen this valley in his imagina-

Drim returned in a car with two missionaries.

"Moi lo can see that he is very sick," whispered Drim, darting a worried glance to Helen Evans, a niece of the Jacksons who was helping them at the tribes center. The tall, dark-haired, dark-eyed young missionary fought back the tears. She hadn't known Sau long, but she heard so much about him, and now he seemed to be almost dead. She helped lift Sau into the car. The frightened little group then drove silently the ten kilometers to the government hospital that sat on one of Dalat's hills.

In the drab ward set aside for tribesmen a doctor examined Sau.

"He suffers from typhoid fever," he said. Drim murmured that he must have picked it up in that distant valley.

Sau lay on a bed of hard boards in a room for the very sick—the death room, the tribespeople called it. Groans came from other patients. The atmosphere was stifling; the smells fetid.

On the second day Sau roused to talk a bit with Drim. After that, sometimes he knew his wife, but sometimes he only stared vacantly as she or Doi or Kar or others of his people or the missionaries bent over him to catch the faintest word concerning his needs.

In a few days he slipped into unconsciousness. For a brief moment they thought he had died.

For almost a month he lay on the hard bed, unaware that his loved ones grieved for his life. One day Drim drew away from the many visitors who crowded the ward. She looked longingly at her husband. As she did his eyelids seemed to flutter. She shed a tear as she wanted to think that his eyes had opened. Then, almost disbelieving, she saw him wide awake.

She cried out. All in the room looked and were startled.

Sau was sitting up!

"Get me water," he said. Several tried to give him a drink.

"Not to drink," he countered. "I must wash my feet."

Days afterward he explained to Drim why this was necessary. He drew her to his bedside. He wanted to tell of a time during his coma when a tremendous surge of life had plumbed the depths of his being. What had been his experience? A dream? An illusion? A vision? Whatever it was, it had taken Sau to the very door of Heaven.

"I traveled a crowded way," he said, closing his eyes to recapture the scene. "Soldiers, Vietnamese women in their graceful gowns, tribesmen in loincloths, white men driving their automobiles—countless travelers jostled one another for position on the wide paved road. My step was heavy and my eyes were weary; I had come a long way. But I thought I heard someone call, and so looked up.

"Beyond the stream of people, by the side of the road, I saw a man standing beside a large, wooden cross.

"For a moment my eyes met his eyes, even across that wide, busy road. Never have I felt such thrill pour through me. How compassionate were those eyes! I stopped in my tracks. I let others brush past me. Then as I strained to hear, I heard the man more clearly."

Drim interrupted. She asked if others heard him, too. Sau opened his eyes as he replied sadly:

"No. They hardly knew that the man was there."

He lifted himself on an elbow and went on.

"The compassionate one said, 'This one is mine.' He pointed to a tribeswoman who wore a black skirt laced with blue thread." She moved toward him.

"Who was she?" asked Drim with interest.

"I did not know her," Sau said. "She was not of our people, but of a tribe that inhabits the plateaus way beyond Dalat's mountains, the ones who call themselves the Raday.

"Her place on the road was swallowed by the throng, as if the gap she left had never really existed at all. A Raday man was called next. Then, to my surprise, *I* was called."

He sat upright.

"Imagine, that the compassionate one should call *me!*"

He lay back, somewhat wearied from the exertion.

"Well," he continued, "I struggled to work across the current to get to the side where the cross stood. I was knocked down and bruised, but it really didn't matter. I finally reached it. There I was with the two who had been called before me.

"Now I could look closely at the man. I tell you, *minoi*, I saw in his face a splendor that I have never seen in all the world. I knew then it had been the splendor, though from afar, and the compassion of his voice that drew me away from the crowd.

"Oh, how reviving it was there, before the cross! I felt my body tingle with new strength. I was about to help the man call others from the road when, without warning, a small door opened in the cross. From it flared a blinding light.

"Now you can be sure that all the travelers took note of the cross

—or, maybe they saw the brilliance that poured through it. More likely the latter. Well, they tried to get to the light. Now they elbowed one another more than they had pushed and bumped each other on the road. No one could enter the open door, however, unless his name was called from within.

"The woman was first to be summoned. As she passed through to the other side, I heard her say, 'God be merciful to me, a sinner.'

"The door closed. I could see now that it was stained with blood. The man from the Raday spoke up while waiting. He had a point he wanted to make clear to all:

" 'It washes sin away.'

"Again the door opened. The man from the Raday was called. And when the door shut the second time—you can believe it!—I found myself inside."

Sau had raised himself up on one elbow. Drim made him lie back before letting him go on. He obeyed only to finish his story.

"I stood on the threshold, and for a while the brightness blinded me. Then slowly I made out objects I could recognize. Before me stretched a boulevard that was wider and straighter than Dalat's. The two whose names had been called—I now saw them dressed in the whitest of robes. They walked the dazzling broad street and seemed to be looking for something.

" 'Here is your house,' I heard a voice tell one of them. Then I saw a villa that put to shame the yellow-plastered houses of Dalat. I saw other houses, some larger, some smaller. And"—he started to sit up again, but under her reproach dropped back—"one was Kar's. But it was not finished.

"Then, in front of another, I saw a placard that bore my own name. But just then a stern voice addressed me.

" 'Why are you in here?' the voice said. 'Why do you seek to enter when there are so many outside needing you?'

"I could only hang my head. Oh, I had an excuse—I was pushed in by the jostling. As you know, ordinarily I speak without waiting to be asked, but that time I had no desire to answer.

" 'Look at you!' the stern voice said to me. I wore no robe like the two Raday, just old black trousers, a threadbare shirt, and a red jacket that had come out of a bundle at the mission.

" 'And look at your feet!' the voice continued. I saw they were bare and heavy with mud from the trail. 'You can't come here with dirty feet.' The feet of those who entered before me glistened as they walked the dazzling street. They were clean. But not mine. I wasn't ready to walk that street. I had come without being ready. And I had come too soon."

Sau's face clouded, then cleared and broke into a faint smile as he went on:

"My place was outside the door, out where the voices had dinned in my ear, where the people were confused and in despair."

On the day that he awoke the doctor said Sau had come back from the brink of death. He would get well. The news spread fast around the tribes center. Many rushed to the hospital to see him alert once again.

"My brother," he said to Kar two days after he had told Drim about his experience, "our houses were not ready. Never mind the houses we have here. We ought to be building on our houses in Heaven."

Nothing on earth rivaled the beauty he had seen, he assured those who came to stand by his bed. But he was saddened—so many ran headlong in their own way that they failed to hear the call of the man at the door to Heaven.

"I have come back to tell people to listen to Him," he said.

9

"Where Will They Move Us?"

WHILE SAU LOUNGED about the yard during his convalescence at the tribes center in Dalat, students at the mission school bombarded him with questions concerning his extraordinary experience. Some were moved by the apparent revelation or vision. Others turned aside to conceal a smile.

"Poor old Sau," they'd say. "His body got well, but what about his mind?"

"That story—" Had any man ever waited on Heaven's doorstep and come back to tell about it?

"Did you really die and go to Heaven?" a student wanted to know.

"I can't be sure," Sau replied. By now he became a little impatient when trying to convince his questioners that his experience was a mystery to him also. "How I saw what I saw, I don't know. I only know that in some way I stood at the door of Heaven."

This spiritual vision had given Sau new insight. Coming back, he underwent a complete change in his heart. Sau, having had the comparison of Heaven, found the splendors of earth tawdry. Never again, he was certain, would the possession of material goods be his goal. True, life had to go on. There would be houses to build and lamps from the market to read by and full rice crops to raise so that bodies could be nourished. But now he looked differently on these worldly things. They would be useful to him in his service to God. No longer would he be a slave to acquiring them.

What, after all, were lamps and china rice bowls? They were transitory. He had more to do than to be taken up by them. There were the eternal souls of men to claim his concern. There were the countless people to reach who had never heard Heaven's call.

He had seen that his spiritual house needed building. He had been given additional time in which to build it. He could drive in a nail by preaching in a needy village. He could put the roof on by faithfully pursuing God's will. Why had it taken a journey to Heaven's doorstep to make him see what his life lacked? But no matter. He saw it.

He felt that the spiritual had won out over the material. It seemed the mud had been washed from his feet. And free from the encumbrance, he now could work for God as he had never worked before.

One bright morning he went out and sat down on a hillside. It was the same hillside that years ago he had helped as a student to terrace. Then and there he made up his mind to echo Christ's call so loudly and clearly and in so many places that those in their mountains could not help but hear it.

But people continued to cast sidelong smiles toward Sau. They did so until one night a missionary to the Raday came from the faraway plateau where the tribe lived. The missionary spoke in the chapel of the tribes center as a guest preacher. K'Sol, who had not heard Sau's story, translated the message into Sau's tongue. The missionary had not heard of Sau's experience, either; so he was surprised at the ripple that swept through the chapel when he told of two Raday believers—a woman and a man—who had died not long ago on the same night.

Following the service the congregation gathered around the missionary to ask on just what night the Raday had died. When he told them, everyone was surprised but Sau. He knew, as he had known all along, that the two passed into Heaven and walked the dazzling street in their spotless robes only moments before he awoke from his long, deep sleep.

His health restored, Sau went back to the mountains. His former efforts at evangelizing were tepid in comparison with those he now put forth. It was as though he had regained that first burst of energy that always came when he was undertaking something new.

He worked as though he had never been sick. When fever or headache struck again or pain plagued his muscles, he refused to pause or give up.

"No, I cannot stay home to nurse my fever," he would say to his wife. "God will take away the ache as I preach—you will see."

Wherever Sau went, he was a magnetic figure. The people knew him as untiring, fearless, zealous in his cause. When they had word that he was coming, they talked about him for days before he arrived. They talked about him for days after he left. While in their presence he entered every conversation. He seemed to dominate the talk, but no one minded, because Sau at heart was a humble man.

Sometimes he preached; more often he spoke informally. He was able to get others to voice their innermost thoughts, too, often leading the pagans to reveal the reasons why some would not give up their old superstitious ways.

"I have heard it said that God-Followers bury their dead in a sitting position," an old-timer once ventured in countering Sau's message. "Because of this I cannot believe."

Others did not question that Jesus once walked the earth, or that the Son was now in Heaven with the Father. But to become a believer—so many had excuses not to do so. Again and again they would say they owed too many sacrifices.

"Someday," a village elder would say, and by his tone emphasize the indefiniteness of the future, "someday, I'll pay my debt to the demons. Then I'll be free to believe."

At this time also the reforms decreed by the government were penetrating to all but the remotest settlements. The teeth-sawing ceremony, for example, was ordered abandoned. Villages made up largely of God-Followers did not find it hard to abide by the stricter laws. In villages where Sau's message had been only partly accepted, divided opinion was evident. The young people with their lives before them were anxious to hear more of the new way. The aged men and the grannies and the sorcerers felt obliged to stick to the old; when the fear and dread which the old engendered became too great, they took to the heady brew of the glazed green jars to forget.

In Viet Nam more tribes were still unreached than had been evangelized. This fact lay heavy on the hearts of Herbert and Lydia Jackson. For many years they had wanted to begin a witness among a belligerent tribe—the Red-Tassel Maa—on the opposite side of Dalat from the Chil. So one day they prepared to leave the tribes center. The separation would be painful. It meant that Sau and his people would see Grandfather and Grandmother only occasionally. But in a moving speech Sau assured his beloved teachers that the lessons they had taught would always remain with the people.

One of these was tithing. A man's gift to the church might be a portion of his crop, or actual piasters he had come by in trade. A woman might share with her pastor's wife the greens she gathered in the forest.

Because the people learned to tithe, they were able to take on most of the support of their pastors, and looked forward to the day when their churches would be financially independent of the mission. The several congregations formed the Tribes Church in 1952. K'Sol was chosen to lead it; Sau was made superintendent of the work around Dalat.

In his travels, Sau often went to Roglai country. A number of other Chil were going that way, too, these days.

Most of Sau's people made the full trip to Howling Water to enjoy fellowship with the Roglai. Their hearts truly went out to their new friends and neighbors. As brothers and sisters they helped the Roglai develop their faith. They saw their efforts rewarded. Within two years of La Yoan's conversion one hundred and six of his tribe were baptized one day in the noisy waters of the Roaring River.

The young couple that Sau had sent them, Doi and his wife, proved to be good ambassadors. The Roglai came to love them. When she gave birth to a child, the women took care of her and the baby and kept house for Doi, not allowing him to lift a hand. In turn, when the Roglai were in trouble, he was able to help them. Smallpox struck, and several died; only the vaccinations Doi gave saved the inhabitants of Howling Water from obliteration.

Traffic between the two tribes moved in both directions. A score of Roglai walked to Mountain Top to help the Chil build a new church. The old building was too small, so Sau designed a structure with two gables side by side. Two dozen men went far into the forest to bring back a huge tree trunk. Split lengthwise, it was scooped out to make an eavestrough between the two sloping roofs.

An unorthodox way to expand the church—but that was Sau.

Occasionally Sau visited his brother among the Tring.

Kar and his wife Gien had found times there hard. As one harvest drew near it seemed that at last they would have a good rice crop. A typhoon, however, swept the steep slopes and they lost it all. Just before another harvest a strong wind destroyed the corn. Where the heathen Tring refused to live together, fearing wrath of evil spirits if they did, tigers attacked the isolated householders. Many people were mauled and eaten.

Kar and Gien by their teaching and example had been God's instruments to bring about great changes.

The Tring learned to work because Kar showed them how. They learned that life could hold laughter when fears dropped away, and there was fun to be found in the games that Kar taught. They learned to pray because they saw in Gien a mother who daily asked God to take the hidden sin from her heart, and to give her patience with the six sons who were constantly under foot, and to keep her from complaining over the shortage of food and the rigors of life in a land that was not her own.

There were three Tring villages now. Young Thanh had come to preach in one and Sieng, a good-looking, bright, but bashful young Chil, in another. People came from long distances to hear the teaching of Kar or Thanh or Sieng.

None walked farther or was more faithful in coming than Ha Rong.

It was Ha Rong who some years ago had thought he might move alongside Kar's house, but refused. Perhaps he had not wanted to become the first to break with the old ways. But now one would never know that he had wavered. In his warmth toward God he left his home every Saturday morning in order to reach Fish Water by nightfall. Sundays he spent at the church in company with the believers. And on Monday mornings he struck out for home. Three days of every week, two of them spent in walking the trail—it was Ha Rong's regular pattern.

True, he was doing what he wanted to do.

"I would stay home and weed my corn if I didn't want to come to church," he said once, and the cords of his long neck grew taut as he spoke. But because he wanted to come, he hardly ever missed. For his earnestness he was made a deacon of the Tring church.

Both Kar and Sau spent brief but frequent periods studying in the school at the tribes center in Dalat. It was hard work, but they were determined to master the books in their language. These few books had been written and put together by one of the missionaries, Myrtle Funé. She and her husband Jean, a Frenchman, had come from the far north of the country after years of missionary service there. Jean now headed the work at the tribes center.

"Dear," Myrtle would say to her husband after a classroom session, "those men try so hard, but I know they'd rather be out among the people teaching what they already know."

Sau got along better in the classes at the mission clinic. There clinic director Evelyn Holiday divided her students into "nurses" and "patients." As a "nurse" Sau would listen to a "patient's" symptoms, then make a diagnosis and prescribe a remedy. If he overdosed a "patient," the teacher would send the poor victim to sit in the "hospital" or even in the "cemetery," an impressive lesson for all the pastors in the class.

Once Sau jumped up from the "hospital," where he was a "patient."

"Pay attention to *moi lo*," he said, sweeping an arm toward the make-believe cemetery. "If I'm sick, I don't want you to put me over there."

Sau sometimes helped Helen Evans, the Jacksons' niece, in translating the Bible into his tongue. At other times he assisted Mrs. Funé and another *moi lo,* Beulah Bowen, who was better known as Peggy. They taught the tribal children living at the center.

Sau and K'Sol were among the first half-dozen men to complete their studies at the tribes Bible school—some twenty years from the time they had begun. After their graduation in December, 1953, came a time of great change in the land.

For years Sau had met jungle men on the trail in his frequent travels to Dalat. But now that he went less often, he found that they, too, were giving up the trail. One day he learned why.

A man in Dalat with whom he struck up a chance conversation said to him:

"The war is nearly over."

Far to the north, the man went on to explain, a long, bloody struggle had raged over a town named Dien Bien Phu. After holding out heroically for two months the French garrison surrendered to the Viet Minh. This foreshadowed the end of colonial rule. Later, the French left the country, taking out not only their soldiers, but their administrators, planters, doctors, and merchants.

The Viet Minh withdrew to the north; they would take the upper half of the country as their own. Thousands opposed to them fled south, where the national government of Viet Nam was to rule. On learning this, Sau smiled.

"At last the guerrillas will leave our mountain forests," he predicted to a friend. "My people will be free of the jungle men's harsh demands."

But the mountain dwellers found that the guerrillas never really did leave. Not all of them, anyway. Some of Ho Chi Minh's fighters remained. Here they formed a hard core of opposition to the national government.

They hid out in the forest, in bands of a dozen or two dozen, keeping always on the move, more like shadows than men of flesh and blood, biding their time as they built up their strength. Officially, the guerrillas were not tied to the Viet Minh government of the north; from what he had seen and heard, however, even in the early days of this new movement, Sau was convinced that these guerrillas could match in brutality every act of their predecessors. In Sau's area they stole what few crops there were, and drove the people's animals into the forest.

The jungle men of this day were called the Viet Cong.

The new looked like the old when they wore the collarless black calico shirts. Some of the men wore black shorts as mates to their shirt. Others dressed in the remnants that had been captured from French or Vietnamese forces—either taken in a raid or snatched from the dead.

Perhaps the outstanding difference between the old and the new lay in the present devotion to a cause, communism. The Viet Cong were thoroughly committed. If the Gospel stood in the way of communism, the new guerrillas, Sau knew, would oppose it bitterly.

There was a method, too, that marked them. Their most effective weapon was infiltration. Any man, in any village, might be one of them.

While this new danger built up, Sau kept on preaching the Gospel. At the same time he was finding new pressures in his personal life.

Sau and Drim now had four sons and two daughters. By tribal custom Sau was often called Father of Sep, after his oldest son. Sep was a problem to his parents. He attended school at the tribes center, but no one could make him behave. He bullied the smaller children with his knife. He imitated the rough characters he saw moving about on a white screen in a building close by Dalat's market. He was unsettled. Maybe it was because of his disappointment in Sep that Sau placed so much hope in Roi, his second son, now twelve.

Roi studied hard; someday he would preach like his father. But one morning Roi was taken from school and sent to the hospital, a very sick boy with a kidney ailment.

For months Roi was in and out of the hospital. Sau spent as much time with his son as possible. He hoped against hope for Roi's recovery until finally he despaired of a cure. He took the swollen, weakened boy home to Mountain Top. As his father had once carried him, a sickly youngster, now Sau bore Roi on his back through the dense forest and up and down the inclines of the path. In the village Roi was alternately sick and well, but a little worse with each recurring spell. Even when sick, however, he couldn't be kept down—there was too much of Sau in him.

"You shouldn't be up, my son," his mother would say as she came into the house and found Roi across the room from his bed.

"I'm looking for my book," he would reply. "I must read the things *moi lo* taught me."

Sometimes his eyes were those of one dead, and he would call deliriously throughout the night. Tenderly the boy's parents would stroke his long curly hair as they kept vigil at his bedside. At other times the boy wanted people to carry him to the chapel, and there he would sit on a backless bench through a very long service.

One day Roi lost consciousness. It seemed like the days of Sau's sickness all over again. Sau said to Drim that soon their son would be walking the bright street that once his eyes had beheld.

"I wonder which of the handsome villas is set aside for this lad," he mused. "Surely, it has to be one of the best."

Sau had come back from the doorstep of Heaven, but Roi's feet were clean. This gentle, good child was ready to live where God lived—what could prevent his going?

Sadly, Sau went into the forest, cut down a tree, and hollowed it out for a coffin. Roi lived a while longer, but his death came as no surprise. Sau wept, of course, but was able to smile through his tears. The tribesmen now had hope in death; no longer did they have to wail in bitter agony and fear for one who had gone on before.

Sau buried him. He wiped his sleeve across his eyes, and comforted Drim. Then he set about his work.

This was a particularly trying time for all of Sau's people. Wind, a severe drought, and a plague of rats combined to wipe out nearly all their crops. Throughout the mountains the Chil people were hungry.

Many would have died, except that gift parcels of food arrived from America in time to save them.

On top of the poverty came harassment by the new breed of jungle men.

In 1956 the new Vietnamese governors of Dalat's province decided on a way to isolate the Viet Cong guerrillas. They would do this by moving whole villages out of the mountains and down to the plains. When the plan became known, the whole tribal population was shaken.

"I have heard that the tribesmen are to be moved out of the mountains," an elder said one day when Sau entered a village to preach.

Sau knew something was up, but had not heard details.

"Where will they move us?" he asked. A picture of the Thach Trai valley flashed suddenly into Sau's mind, and he hoped that this could be the place.

"Yes, where will they move us?" the old man said in utter bewilderment.

Sau decided to learn more of the plan. On a visit to Dalat he was told that the mountain people were to be moved to flat lands down from Dalat and toward the sea. This change from the limitless mountain slopes to the smaller plain would bring a drastic new way of living. Not all could have fields of their own—there wouldn't be room. Some would be taken off the land to learn a new type of weaving and the making of many strange things. Some would have to hire themselves out, a practice Sau's people abhorred. Of those who did plant, some would raise food the tribesmen had never tasted. Others would grow rice in flooded fields. It was this that brought the uproar.

Wet rice fields? Not for a Chil or Tring or Roglai. Mountaineers knew only how to pierce the earth with a stick, to drop in a seed, and then to watch the earth give them a crop. And to eat wet rice? They would rather grub for leaves and roots.

Sau was at first disturbed by the plan, but as he traveled from village to village he came across tribesmen who were violent in their opposition.

"The bones of our ancestors are buried here," said one man angrily, and a dozen voices joined his in bitter denunciation. It would be courting disaster, they said, to abandon the graves of those who had died.

"We roof them over to keep off the rain," one said. "But left alone, the roofs will rot. The rain will fall on the graves. In his cold, wet misery the soul of the dead one will then seek his revenge against us."

The government turned a deaf ear to their pleas.

Tension mounted.

Some suspicious tribesmen saw trickery involved.

"Now that the yellow man rules in Dalat in place of the French, does he intend to take our land for himself?" one or another would ask.

"Perhaps we'd do better to listen to the jungle men," others remarked. "It is not they who are asking us to leave our homes."

In the spring of 1957 the government called men from the seething villages to a meeting near the old French *poste* that Sau's people passed on the way to town. Sau, who spoke languages with ease, and who was now ordained in the Gospel ministry and recognized as a leader by government and tribes, was called on to interpret the officials' talk.

"We cannot allow you people to live where the guerrillas can reach you. We will move you to the flat lands where we can protect you."

Sau quoted the government order to the vast throng. An angry rumble drowned out his voice. Some failed to understand that the voice was Sau's, but not the words; they blamed Sau for what he said. On the edge of the crowd two men who appeared to be no more than interested spectators listened carefully, making mental notes of what Sau was saying. When they had heard enough to form a report, they slipped away before the meeting broke up. Back into the jungle they went, deep into the forest, to a secret headquarters. There they informed their black-clad chiefs that one Sau, a leader of the God-Followers, had said the people should move to a place where the guerrillas could not reach them.

The words had not been Sau's when he spoke them, but later as he heard of this village or that being increasingly troubled by the jungle men, and as he recalled the recent sad days of famine, he wondered if all of the tribesmen ought not go.

But why to the flooded flat lands? Why not to Thach Trai, the good valley, where the soil had been fine to his taste and he had envisioned a new home for his people. That broad land of great forests and rolling hills would grow the dry rice they wanted; the guerrillas would not plague them here. To Sau, no place of refuge beckoned like Thach Trai.

Before he could suggest it in place of the government plan he began to hear talk that frightened him. Through what he heard, he knew that conflict between the old and new ways was about to erupt. The discussion always revolved around the impending move. "We who worship the evil spirits know only the gods of the mountains," said men and their wives and the old grannies in the pagan settlements he visited. "We're afraid of the spirits of the flat lands more than we are afraid of those in the mountains. We don't know how to appease *them*."

"It is better to die in the mountains than to live where the rivers flood," cackled a toothless old woman. Her words brought forth a torrent of wailing from those who sat with her at the alcohol jars.

They became the cry that swept along every trail—village to village —"die in the mountains!"

So the government had its plan to move them, did it? Well, a handful of spirit worshipers came up with a plan of their own by which they would never have to live on a flooded plain. Quickly, the scheme spread. It was this artful design that lifted Sau's heart to his mouth.

The village elders had dispatched a messenger to the government offices in Dalat. "We want you to come to view our sacrifice," he said. "The tribesman insists that his yellow master come."

The plan involved a sacrifice feast. Spread over many days, even weeks, it would start with chickens, continue with pigs, and end up with water buffalo. When one last animal remained in each village, and every member of that village was present, the elder would poison the last buffalo and the choppers and spearers would kill it. And on that final, nearly raw sacrifice every man, woman, and child would feast until he died an agonizing death.

They had planned their revenge. They would die at the feet of horrified officials.

This was an ancient method of registering a protest. No doubt the old women, whose time was running out anyway, had dredged it from deep in their memories and, true to custom, the sons were obeying the voices of their mothers.

Sau came upon villages in which preparation for the suicidal orgies had begun. No God-Follower was involved. But thousands of his fellow tribesmen would die. He was alarmed, as once before the certain death of his people had alarmed him. These people did not know the God of Heaven. They weren't ready to die!

Yet, he knew that the eating of the animals had started. The massive feast was progressing toward the final deadly morsel.

10

The Day of Exodus

IN A PAGAN VILLAGE not far from Mountain Top, the prolonged sacrificial feast was in its final stages. Suddenly, a courier arrived from Dalat. He called the villagers together and addressed them.

"Don't poison your buffalo!" he shouted, and produced a paper bearing the official cachet.

The villagers thought he had come to witness their deaths, so they resented his interference with their plans. Then he cried out:

"There is no reason to kill yourselves! This paper says you do not have to move from the mountains."

Resentment gave way to jubilation. The villagers brought out their alcohol jars. Other couriers appeared at other villages. Word spread quickly through the mountains that the order to move to the flatlands had been canceled.

Unlike the spirit worshipers around them, the people of Mountain Top, although they did not intend to move, had no idea of doing away with themselves by eating poisoned buffalo. They turned instead to the task of putting up a new house for God.

They replaced their two-gabled church with still a larger one, this time a building with three gables side by side and a metal roof.

Sau said this church should be as strong as their faith; he led them to a spot in the forest two days away to get sturdy posts. The logs were so long that it took twenty men to carry each one back to the crest of the mountain and put it into place. For the sides, the men brought bamboo. They sliced the long stems and wove them into a basket pattern.

The roof was to require self-denial on the part of every family. Sau estimated they would need one hundred eighty sheets of corrugated iron. Each family agreed to pay its share of the cost. Some, however, had no way of paying except by going to Dalat and, swallowing pride, hiring themselves out until they had earned the money. Having bought their portion, they joined the others in shouldering the heavy sheets to carry them for two days along the slippery mountain trails to Mountain Top.

The new church was built in two months; the villagers looked at it with pride. Now they had another reason for staying where they were.

On hearing that the order for the tribesmen to move had been rescinded, Sau felt great joy. But it was short-lived. He knew their days in the mountains were numbered.

He believed this because he had seen the evidence. In his travels he kept hearing of more demands, of more threats, and of more raids by the Viet Cong. Just recently the rebels, now pressing their guerrilla warfare desperately, had put three villages to the torch. When they first appeared, they sought to persuade, yes; but not for long. Village leaders who resisted their blandishments and objected to their tactics had been summarily killed.

"They have taken our sons!" wailed the grannies in one village the day after all the young men had been marched into the forest for indoctrination by the guerrillas. "Next they will come to take away the last of our rice and corn and we will all die."

Sau called together his friends at Mountain Top to tell them what he had seen and heard.

"Some night this will happen to us!" he warned. A few nodded their heads in agreement, but none was sufficiently excited to think they should seek another area.

Sau learned that the government, determined to isolate the guerrillas, was preparing once more to move the villagers to the plains. This time it would act quietly and quickly before new protests could be raised. His own people would be moved; it was only a matter of time.

A few weeks later he was asked to escort a party of missionaries from Dalat through Mountain Top to Tring country, down through the Roglai settlements, and by river to the coast. He learned that they would pass through the valley known as Thach Thai. The prospect filled him with anticipation. He was disappointed that Grandfather and Grandmother could not come. They were busy making plans for starting a witness among the Red-Tassel Maa. But others from the tribes center dear to his heart were coming, including K'Sol, whom he had not seen for some time. Ong Loc, the district chief of Nha Trang, accompanied them; he was a man of genuine warmth who regarded the tribespeople of his district with respect; he also felt obligated to look out for the Americans, so he brought a few soldiers along.

The presence of the Viet Cong in the country through which they would pass made the journey dangerous. Physically, however, travel over the trail was not so hard as it might have been, thanks to the work that Sau, Kar, La Yoan, and others had already done.

Loc grew to admire Sau. He liked this tribeman's ingenuity, his ambition, his attitude. He thought the improvements he had engineered on the trail remarkable. He was impressed most at Mountain Top where Sau had the last season's Christmas pageant repeated for his guests.

"Think of the detail this man and his people put into this program —away out here in these mountains!" Loc exclaimed.

Sau enjoyed the trip, but above all, the hours spent in the Thach Trai valley. They were getting ready to board bamboo rafts for the trip downriver to the coast, when he asked Jean Funé his opinion as to whether the people of Mountain Top should move. Funé, so placid for a Frenchman, thoughtfully fingered his mustache before replying:

"You will have to move someday," he said. "If you move before the government makes you, then you can go to a place of your own choosing."

Sau next sought out Nam. "Do *you* think we ought to move to this valley?" he asked. Nam, now a teacher at the tribes center, had shown himself to be a real friend of the tribesmen.

"This is a good place," Nam said.

"But it is hot, not like the cool of our mountains," Sau countered.

"The soil looks good, and the heat will raise you much food," Nam offered.

"The mosquitoes will bring us sickness," Sau replied.

"Men in your village have been trained to fight the mosquito," Nam rejoined.

"The people don't want to move," Sau said.

"You are their leader," Nam declared with finality.

Sau's own doubts were settled once and for all. The answers Nam gave were the answers Sau had been giving to others. He only needed reassurance that he was right.

He saw it all very clearly.

Years ago God had kept the Chil and Roglai from killing each other. More recently the Roglai, like the Chil before them, had been brought under the covenant of Christ's blood. From it the Roglai gained a new and happy life; from the resulting friendship between the two tribes the Thach Trai valley opened up as a place of refuge just when the people of Mountain Top were needing it.

Now perhaps he was ready for the next step. Sau knew that thousands of Roglai lived in the mountains that loomed on three sides of Thach Trai. Unlike the Chil, most of them had not had an opportunity to believe in the God of Heaven. If many God-Followers came to live in the valley—not just Chil, but also the Roglai of Howling Water—the Gospel could be taken into the mountains with a mighty thrust.

Maybe the Tring would come to the valley, too. He recalled having talked about this with Kar when the missionary party had stopped in Fish Water village.

"Our people need to leave these barren peaks," Kar had said. "Our crops have failed again, and once more the Tring are hungry." He added that he was aware the guerrillas were moving closer to them all the time.

"Will the God-Followers of the Tring be willing to leave the place of their ancestors?" Sau asked.

"They will—most of them," Kar replied. "I cannot be sure of them all." As he thought about it, he added, "In fact, I cannot be sure of any of them."

That handsome, engaging talker among them, the deacon Ha Rong, was the one responsible for Kar's uncertainty.

Ha Rong had long been discontented. He talked about leaving his stony field to seek a better fortune elsewhere. But when the government ordered the tribesmen to move, he did an about-face and was among the most defiant in his opposition.

Vacillating Ha Rong was a problem for Kar. On occasion he exhibited great zeal—as when he walked all day to get to church. But increasingly, he seemed to be eaten up by bitterness. Many things, many people, were bringing it out in him these days. Yet he had lost none of his persuasiveness, and if Ha Rong were to stand up some Sunday in church and speak against the move, his words might have great effect.

"Who can ever tell about Ha Rong?" asked Kar.

Once back from the trip Sau was pressed by many duties. One day he was called to Saigon, the capital city, to represent the Chil at the celebration of Viet Nam's independence. On his first day there he met Loc, the official who had accompanied them through tribal country.

Loc invited Sau to come with him to his temporary quarters in a government office. They entered a big tawny building in which countless clerks bent over countless desks.

"*Niam sa*—Is your body good?" Loc asked. He used the tribesman's greeting he had learned on the trip. He took Sau's hand in both of his and led him to a less bustling corner near a window. He asked Sau to sit down. Sau wondered at this; a tribesman never sat in the presence of a government official.

For several minutes Loc engaged in polite talk. Sau tried to remember the niceties of Oriental culture he had learned over the years in Dalat. Finally, Loc came around to what he had to say.

"As a district chief," he declared, "I invite you to become a member of my staff."

So that was it! The man was offering him a government post. Immediately, Sau knew this would be impossible. He already had a job—working for the God of Heaven. He wanted to say "no" right then, but Loc talked on.

"I will make you the chief of all the tribespeople in my district. There are untold numbers of your people living in my mountain area, and you will represent me to them."

Sau frowned. Loc thought he did not understand.

"When I wish to speak to the tribes," he explained, "I will speak to you, and you will pass my word on to the people. And in keeping with the democracy of our government, you in turn will tell me what the tribesmen want."

Sau tried to grasp what this would mean. He was being offered a position of importance almost unheard of for a tribesman, a place of power, of trust, of responsibility. In the new day that was coming, he would be a big man. And he would be well paid. As though reading his thoughts, Loc said, "I offer you three thousand piasters a month."

Sau said nothing.

"Four thousand."

"No," Sau said quietly.

"You will have ten soldiers under you and civil servants, too."

But Sau only shook his head.

Loc, surprised at Sau's reaction, raised his voice a pitch.

"Friend," he said, "many people have offered me their buffalo and rice crop for appointment to my staff. But I am asking nothing of you. Do you understand? I am not asking you to buy a place in my office. I am inviting you to come."

Sau looked out of the window at the sea of people on the city streets. He studied them—the men in their Western business suits, the young girls in their high satin collars and cone-shaped hats, the peasant women carrying heavy but balanced loads on their shoulders by means of *ghan* sticks, the monks in saffron robes, the boyish soldiers who nervously fingered their guns. They were going on their way so unheeding. Yet every one of them needed to hear that Christ was calling them to enter through the Cross. Unless someone told them, would they ever know?

Here was a job—to bring the world to Jesus Christ!

"I'm a preacher," said Sau. "I'll always be a preacher."

Loc stood up. He paced for a while as Sau sat silently. Then he drew his chair close to Sau's and sat down again.

"My friend," he said, "what do you get out of your preaching? Certainly not money. But just what does it give you? Be realistic."

He got to his feet again. Sau's eyes followed this man who was trying so hard to get him to change his mind.

"You've tried to get the people to move," Loc said. "But they turn a deaf ear to your pleading. You spend days and nights on the trail. Sometimes you don't see your family from one week to the next. Why go on wearing yourself out? And what thanks do you get for it? Do these savage sacrificers in the mountains appreciate your message? Aside from a handful. Tell me. Do they?"

Sau did not answer.

"Just think," Loc went on, "what authority I can give you, what prominence. You may never get such a chance again."

Sau thought a minute.

"My answer," he said, mustering all his strength, "is no. It will always be no."

Riding the bus back from Saigon, Sau thought over the interview. He of course could not accept Loc's offer. He was a preacher and he'd always be one. But he had to admit that there was much truth in what Loc said. He *was* wearing himself out. He *was* away from his family much of the time. A question came to him: Could he not serve God just as well by stopping all this traveling about, by settling in one village, there to be the spiritual leader of friends who might appreciate him?

To reach his home in the mountains he had to go through Dalat. This afforded him opportunity to brush aside, for a few days, the disturbing uncertainties. He went immediately to the tribes center. He sought out the houses in which families stayed when they came in from the hills for marketing. There he enjoyed himself again in the fellowship around the fires of friends.

Then on the eve of his departure for home he remembered that he had not yet visited the *moi lo* as he usually did to tell them of his plans for the days ahead. He could not leave without doing so.

He went across the compound to their home. He found Helen Evans alone, engrossed in translation work.

This niece of the Jacksons was rather tall; she had dark hair and eyes—like tribeswomen. She was one to appreciate the ways of the tribes, having gained insight through mastering the language. Because she spoke his tongue and had such heart for his people, Sau felt completely at ease in talking with her.

"You look troubled," said *moi lo*.

No sooner had they sat down than the weariness, the unanswered questions, the uncertainties flooded over him.

"I've come to a decision," Sau replied somewhat abruptly. "I want to give up being the superintendent of our church. I don't want to travel any more. I want to settle down to one village church like other men who preach."

Moi lo did not conceal her surprise.

"Someone has been talking to you," she said.

He did not reply.

"I'm sure you would make a fine pastor of one church if you limited yourself to just one. But"—she smiled faintly—"I think I know you better than you know yourself. I think I can say you will never be content to settle down to one church. You will always go where the Gospel has not been preached. I know it and you know it."

Sau grinned. She was right. What he wanted was not to occupy himself with a single parish when he felt responsible for all the parishes of their mountains, but to be free of all the demands that took him away from God's work. Right now, he wanted more time to preach to the Roglai.

"I don't want to stop serving God wherever God wants me," he replied. "I want to work for God until I die—and I will. I always carry a suit of clothes in my basket in case I die on the trail. I don't know when I might die, but when I do I'll have a suit to be buried in."

Sau left Dalat with a lighter heart.

The savage war with the Viet Cong now called for all the villages to move.

All over the land brother was fighting brother. Trusted village officials in the daytime became accomplices of the enemy by night. Children wandered innocently into mined fields and were blown to bits. No one could be sure about tomorrow, or tonight—or even today. Sau thought his people should leave as soon as possible. He ought to take them beyond the enemy's reach.

He argued and pleaded and coaxed some more: one day, to his surprise, they agreed to go.

Once they had made up their minds, they would not be held back. Not only the villagers of Mountain Top but the God-Followers in Chil settlements around them made their preparations. Parties went on ahead to Thach Trai, first to slash and burn big patches of forest, then to plant new fields and to clear an area extending some two hundred meters back from the river for a village.

Finally the day of the exodus came.

The people of Mountain Top were the first to go, though a few decided to stay on. Each family stripped its field and packed the corn and a few sweet potatoes in baskets. All those able to walk loaded themselves with blankets and mats, rice bowls, gongs, chickens, young children, and precious copies of Bible translations and hymns. Helped by two dozen dogs, they drove their goats and pigs before them as they walked single file over the rugged trail, having abandoned their houses and beloved church to the care of those who remained.

To some it was the first evacuation in this shadowy war with communist guerrillas. To Sau it was the march of a victorious army; they were on their way to peace, enjoying deliverance from a human foe, and also from their natural enemies—cold wind, frost, and rocky ground.

But as they moved the first signs of danger were already visible. The day before they left Mountain Top word came from the Viet Cong forbidding the people to go.

"What you are about to do, they are afraid others will also do," a furtive visitor said to Sau. "The jungle men do not like your going beyond their reach.

"But it is you they hold responsible," the visitor added. "They know you are the leader."

Sau asked what the guerrillas intended to do.

"I bring you their warning," said the informant. "If you lead your people away, they will kill you."

But here they were, Sau and his people, pushing forward happily in spite of the obstacles of the trail. They gave scant thought to the threats of the jungle men. There seemed to be a new closeness among them as in late afternoon men helped women gather wood for their campfires and perform other chores that once they would not have done; an unbreakable bond of love was evident as at night, mustered near the fires for protection against tigers, they took advantage of being together to fill the forest with prayers and praises to God.

Sau's people arrived in the Thach Trai valley in June, 1957. Two months later other believers from the Chil tribe came from a scattering of villages to join them. Many built family houses, rather than longhouses for whole clans, in the prepared clearing. This village of nearly six hundred persons they called Jong Lo, meaning Chinese Foot, though why this name had been chosen, no one knew.

About this time Kar brought in several hundred God-Followers from four Tring villages. Kar and Gien carried a newborn, as they had when they went to the land of the Tring nearly nine years before. It was a boy, their tenth child, and this young life might have been a symbol of the new life that lay ahead for the Tring.

Sau was on hand to greet the Tring as they arrived. He welcomed them gladly, telling them the valley was big enough to hold all who would come. The Tring settled in three villages, none of them much more than a half-hour's walk from Jong Lo.

Kar's Fish Water people decided on a site upstream from Jong Lo and on the same side of the river as the Chil. Another group led by the young preacher Sieng went directly to the other side of the river opposite Jong Lo. The third, whose pastor was a man named Poh, went across the river at Kar's place and up a small tributary stream. Kar's village was named Sim Jong, meaning Bird Foot; Sieng's they called Da Mham, or Blood River; Poh's, Da Mur, which meant Underground River.

The people of Thanh's church were among those who came, but they scattered among the three Tring villages in the valley and Thanh was assigned a pastorate elsewhere.

In just a few months Doi brought a large group of Roglai into the valley. They built their village—a new Howling Water—near their Chil friends, perhaps a fifteen-minute walk from Jong Lo.

Sau was delighted. This once taboo valley was now home to nearly eighteen hundred persons of three tribes. Their dialects and traditions varied; not many years before they lived in suspicion, avoiding each other. Now they were one family, enjoying an eager new spirit of co-operation, worshiping one God. Their houses were not yet much more than lean-to's, and the church in each village was only a temporary shelter. But prospects for the future were good; never better, it seemed to Sau.

All shared his optimism; all, that is, with one exception. Ha Rong, the Tring deacon, the changeable one, had put up his house at Da Mur, the village farthest from the center of community life. It was a bad choice, he said, though he made no effort to change his location. It seemed he would rather be in a position to complain that his land was not so good as the land of the others than to do anything about it.

"In the mountains my field contained rock and thin soil," he said somewhat bitterly in Kar's presence one evening. "Here I have nothing but rock and dry sand. What have we gained by our move?"

And, too, Ha Rong had not realized how hot it would be here. Constantly, he reminded the people how nice it had been to sleep by their fires on a cool night in the mountains. How attractive he could make the old days sound!

He was a man with an unhappy spirit, always dissatisfied. Yet, he had been eager to come. Some days he wanted to be here in the valley, some days he didn't. He blew hot, then cold.

"Ha Rong is a persuasive talker," Kar said to Sau one day after they heard him stir the people with his complaints.

"But when he's not talking he's a brooding man," added Sau.

They agreed that if anyone could bring trouble to their Eden, it would be Ha Rong.

11

Hardly Worth Gathering In

THE FIRST CROP at Thach Trai was disappointingly poor, hardly worth gathering in under the blistering sun.

"Something must be seriously wrong," said a fretful old villager to Sau after a discouraging day in the field. "We planted more rice and corn than we ever did at Mountain Top, but what we have cut will not last out the winter."

"Don't be sad, uncle," Sau replied. "When the rice runs out we'll eat the fruit that our gardens will then be giving."

Maybe they hadn't timed their planting right with the wet monsoon, he thought. Even the rains in this valley were strange, coming at a different season and from a different direction, all so unlike the old familiar rains of their mountains. Perhaps before the move the advance parties hadn't worked hard enough to prepare the land.

"Next year . . ."

Sau was reassuring; his smile and contagious optimism made the future appear much brighter, as he directed the planting of new fields and the building of more substantial homes. Under his exacting eye the men laid out straight rows of banana trees and pineapple plants, although they could not understand why their old way of hit-or-miss was not good enough.

"You're not on the steep slope of a mountain now," Sau would say as the men worked to put in sugar cane, corn, squash, manioc, gourds, and tropical fruits, as well as mountain rice. "The vegetable growers at Dalat plant straight rows and the ground gives them an abundant yield."

It was the same with their houses. Sau laid out a straight street in Jong Lo, and before a man dug the post holes for his house, he measured from the street with a stick that Sau provided. Other villages were laid out with similar care.

In each village the church was prominent. It looked to the villagers like a mother hen, and their houses, whether up on posts or squat on the ground, like chicks. Although the fields had been hacked out of virgin forests, few trees remained in the clearing. Paths connected the three villages on one side of the river, and canoes provided a crossing to the other two.

They had not been in the valley long before Sau saw the need for bridges. In the approaching wet season a crossing by canoe could become hazardous if the river rose suddenly.

Sau consulted with Kar. The brothers planned to build two of them, one to connect Kar's Sim Jong with Da Mur; the other to provide a crossing downstream between Sau's Jong Lo and Da Mham. They called men from all the villages to work on them.

At Sim Jong a monkey bridge was anchored to giant trees and hung from one high bluff to another. Testing it, Sau spread his arms and barely touched the sides; he took twenty sweeping strides to walk its length. The bamboo floor bounced under his step, but he noticed the sagging middle stayed clear of the current beneath.

"A good bridge," Sau said, coming back to the hundred people who lined Sim Jong's high bank to await his pronouncement. Then he frowned. "We'll see if it is still good enough when the rain swells the river."

Downstream at Jong Lo the banks were not quite so high. Here a small island divided the river, making it possible to build this bridge of logs with its center resting on the island. The crews then turned their attention to a road. Once put in shape, the road could be traveled by a horse or a truck along the river all the way back to Da Mham.

A new era dawned for the peoples of Thach Trai.

Their bridges built, their houses going up, their plantings beginning to show fresh and green, the people on both sides of the river now visited back and forth freely. The villages were only minutes apart; and the bridges and jungle paths connecting them soon became well-traveled routes—Chil mingled with Roglai, Tring with Chil, Roglai with Tring. Distinction between the groups seemed to be fading. Five villages, each with a cross of bamboo instead of a sacrificial mast reaching toward the sky, each with different backgrounds and traditions, were living together as peaceful, friendly neighbors.

In the months that followed Sau often walked those well-trodden paths. Every church frequently called on him to preach. He gave out medicine, taught children to read, and checked on the progress of various projects in each community. Sometimes he made the rounds just to chat with the local pastors.

One day, while taking the path that led away from the river to Da Rom, the new home of the people from Howling Water, he came upon Doi quietly directing the Roglai in the construction of a fine new church. It made Sau feel good to visit in this village. It had been only six years since some of the Roglai wanted to kill their first God-Follower, La Yoan; now with dedication they built a house for God that was much better than any of their own.

Upon his return to Jong Lo, Sau joined a group of young men playing the gongs. A skilled gonger himself, he was helping them to produce the resonant tones that sometimes resembled the muffled rumble of a distant waterfall, sometimes the lively skipping of a melodious stream. Sau enjoyed playing the gongs, and also the plaintive gourd pipes.

After a while he stopped. But he noticed that the others did not. They went right on playing. Among them was Jao, the young preacher who filled Sau's pulpit when he was away. Then it struck Sau that the gong players—Jao included—never wanted to stop. They wanted to play on and on. They wanted to do nothing but play. He should have been aware of this before. This was symbolic—a symptom of the laxness that overcame his own Chil people. He pulled himself up suddenly and began to think.

How many entered the church every morning to pray? How many families sang hymns around their fires at night? Very few, he had to admit.

Late one afternoon he pried his understudy from the biggest of the brass disks and led him to the shade of a house. They sat on the small veranda and leaned against the doorposts.

"We ought to make improvements on our church," Sau prodded the play-loving Jao, not scolding, but speaking forcefully as a father would. "The roof needs repair and we could use more benches."

Jao was still an overgrown boy, clever, intelligent, and with a captivating personality, yet he was inclined to be lazy. Beneath this surface, however, he had a love for God and the people, and Sau believed he had potential. Jao sat slumped forward, his eyes closed. Sau knew the youth was not being impudent; it was his way when thinking deep thoughts.

"You are troubled," Sau said.

Jao was slow to speak, but Sau waited him out by drumming his fingers on his knees to the timing of the distant gongs.

"The people don't much like to work," Jao said finally, straightening his back and looking at Sau.

"They don't like to work, and they don't work." There was some bitterness in Sau's voice.

"They're hot and they're tired," Jao answered. "Some are sick and all are sad."

Sau tried to see things from their point of view. He knew that many lay languid on the hard wooden beds they had made when building their houses. They complained that their heads ached from the hot days and from the nights that were cooler than the days but which held a warmth so different from the cold night air of the mountains. Sau, too, found the days and nights uncomfortable, but sweating and aches and weariness had not kept him from working.

Yet as Jao recounted the ills of the people Sau could not help but sympathize with them. He knew full well that some burned with fever and had not responded to the pills he gave them. His heart went out to them. It was here that he had contracted his own grave illness. He reminded himself that they were in this hot, parched valley because he had brought them here. He did not hold it against them that they blamed him for their plight.

Nevertheless, he was disappointed that some were not content to wait for the new crop and for the cooling rains to come. Everything would turn out all right, he was sure, if they'd just exercise a little patience—have a little faith.

Sau got to his feet. Before walking over to the church to see what had to be done, he looked down at Jao, who had again slumped down as if he were asleep.

"Are people so sick and so sad," he asked, "that they can't call on God to help them?"

This time Jao did not reply.

Often in his rounds of the villages Sau sought out his brother Kar. None had worked harder in their fields than the Sim Jong people who came from the old Tring village of Fish Water. Kar did a fine job in teaching them to work, and also to laugh and play. For some time Kar flashed a white smile, showing off the new dentures that filled the void from the teeth-sawing ceremony of his youth. At the market or at the mission he chose clothes that had a dash of color. Handsome Kar was a peacock in appearance, but in conduct a humble man who was everyone's friend. He remained cheerful when nobody else saw any reason for being cheerful. If the smile slipped from Sau's face he found no one could bring it back as Kar could.

But in these days of the hot, dry season in the Thach Trai valley even Kar did not often smile.

"So many are sick from the bite of the mosquito," he said to Sau on one of the latter's visits. "And our people are hungry."

The brothers walked out to Kar's field. A tiny bamboo hut stood perched on log legs in a tract of corn. Kar led the way up the notched pole and into the storehouse.

"My corn is nearly gone," Kar said with a sigh, pointing to a small heap in a corner of the house. "The rice our people gave as tithe we shared with them last week."

Sau noted only a few squash in the middle of the floor and some spare clothing Kar had hung in the storehouse to make more room in his village house for his large family. Sau knew that the people of Sim Jong were hungry—and that those of Jong Lo and Da Mur and the other villages were also hungry. Sau himself was hungry. He woke up hungry and he went to bed hungry. Following his brother now down the steps, he glanced at his belt. It was slack again; he'd have to punch another hole in it.

But one of these days he'd loosen it. Soon the corn would be in, and from the looks of Kar's field there would be corn for all. Then everything would be all right. The people would forget these days of misery.

If he could just get them to hang on a bit longer. As they walked down the rows, Kar talked of his crop.

"The stalks are tall," he said, pointing to the green leaves that reached as high as their shoulders. Kar stripped an ear from a stalk. It was big, and Sau saw there were many such ears in the field. For weeks he had been watching the corn grow and felt a pride that his own brother's was the best-looking in all the valley.

"The ear is big"—Kar peeled back the husks for Sau to see—"but only because the cob is big."

Hardly a kernel on it had developed.

Sau was stunned. He had based his conviction that his people's hunger would soon be over on the evidence of the growing corn. Those tempting big ears he had thought of as the mark of abundance. They had deceived him. Had he deceived himself?

Had he deceived the hundreds who with simple trust followed him here?

He recalled that in the day of the python goddess the sorcerer had limited the people to eating one kernel of corn a day. Well, now, they had hardly more than that here, and this time the lack could not be laid at the door of evil spirits.

In a few days Sau walked down the steep bank at Sim Jong to cross over the bamboo bridge to the path that led to Da Mur. This was the one untidy, haphazardly built village of the five. Here he found the people listless, worn out spiritually as well as physically. And as in the other places, many burned with fever.

He came expressly to see Ha Rong's wife, who, he had heard, was very ill. Sau found her thin and wasted, her eyes bloodshot, her forehead hot to his touch.

Ha Rong came in. Sau said to him that he would like to pray.

"Pray if you like," said Ha Rong with a shrug, but it was evident from his tone that he himself did not intend to. Sau looked hard at Ha Rong. Some curious change had come over him.

"She needs rest," Sau said after he had finished.

Ha Rong turned on him.

"And when she sleeps who will cook my supper?" he demanded. He sat down on the edge of his wife's bed. Sau saw his face had become a bitter mask, the mouth, the eyes, the flaring nostrils all reflecting a rancorous spirit; the cords stood out in his long neck.

"Supper . . ." Ha Rong muttered. "Why do I speak of supper?"

He stood up and bowed mockingly to Sau.

"Stay, and we'll have stones for supper."

The next harvest was also meager. "What do you lay it to *this* time?" several asked Sau scornfully. Most families went into the forest to search for edible roots and leaves. In former years they had made up for smallness of the harvests by the help of such fare. Why not again? Some, however, could not find any. They complained that they did not know the jungle so well in this place. They did not know whether their kinds of leaves and mushrooms grew in this intolerably hot climate. Others refused to go to the forest to find out. Sullenly, they waited for Sau to find some way to feed them.

One day young pastor Thanh brought rice to augment the valley's low supply. The people were full of gratitude. But what were a dozen or so baskets of grain for nearly eighteen hundred empty stomachs?

The following Sunday Sau was walking toward the church a few minutes before the evening service was to start, when he met a man going in the opposite direction. The man avoided Sau's gaze; in answer to Sau's greeting he said apologetically, "I won't be going to the meeting in God's house."

"Why not?" asked Sau.

"Because I have had to go far in the forest today to find food for my family."

"Did God help you find the food?" Sau asked, noticing that the basket on the man's back was filled with leaves.

"Yes," he said sullenly. "But I'll thank God another day when I'm not so tired."

The complaints grew louder and more frequent. Nearly every conversation now included Sau's name. Some upheld him, reminding others that he had been a wise leader through the years—that he had suffered with them. But in many a house his name was spoken only with bitterness and contempt.

One morning a group from Jong Lo announced:

"We're going home!"

"Home" meant the mountains—windswept, rocky, and cold, now nearly altogether controlled by the marauding guerrillas of the rebel Viet Cong. The conditions awaiting them back there didn't matter; they had made up their minds they were going.

These were Chil people. Sau had known them all as friends. A few had come from Mountain Top, the others from settlements close to Sau's former village. Many had been the nights he sat at their fires and taught them what the Bible said. That made no difference now. They despised him.

While only a handful of Tring and Roglai prepared to go, nearly four hundred of the six hundred Chil announced they were leaving the valley. A number of them went to Sau's house to vent their rage. They stalked into the big room, where he sat at a table with his family, eating stewed leaves.

"We're going now," a man said angrily. He was one with whom Sau had often prayed.

"I wish you would not," Sau answered softly.

"We were happy back there," another said.

Were they? Sau wondered. Had they forgotten how often in the mountains they were hungry? He recalled the time that whole villages would have died had not the Americans sent them food. Yet he could remember no grumbling in those days. But then, unlike now, they had no one on whom to blame their misfortune.

"Why did you make us come?" one in the crowd demanded.

"Yes, it was your idea to move here," another said.

Once Sau might have argued with them, with temper flaring and the words spewing out rashly. But now he said nothing, did nothing. He only stared emptily into the bowl of murky leaves.

Their invective finally waned and Sau spoke. He beseeched them to stay.

"The mountain rice has begun to sprout," he said, and he could not suppress a smile of optimism. "The Roglai will give us new seed that produces good corn in this warm climate."

An angry old woman cut him short. Spitefully, she hurled her words at him:

"Before another harvest we'll all be dead! Aren't our heads burning with fever and our stomachs empty?"

"You lied to us," a man cried out accusingly. They all joined in, their voices rising in angry chorus: "We hate you! We hate you! We hate you!"

Cursing, threatening, the dissatisfied ones left, their screams trailing back as they took the path out of the village and out of the valley. Sau, still sitting at the table, bowed his head; he cracked the knuckles of his fingers and ran a hand through the blue-black curls. Again he stared at the bowl of leaves before him. Hungry though he was, he could not eat.

There still were nearly fourteen hundred men, women, and children in the valley. They felt uncertain, apprehensive, perhaps somewhat petulant toward Sau, but they were willing to risk staying, willing to see if God could really provide.

Their trials, however, were far from over.

Kar managed to bring in a fairly good harvest in one of his fields. Then one night he was awakened by a crackling sound. He looked out to see his storehouse, where he had put his harvest, in flames.

All his corn was destroyed.

To the villagers this was another hope dashed. Then at the very depths of their despair, Doi's people sent over a few baskets of rice from Da Rom. This kindness deeply moved the people of Sim Jong.

"From their little the Roglai gave to us," they said with awe.

Kar was also happy when he found that his gongs had not been in the storehouse, but in his house, and so escaped destruction.

A man whom Sau knew came one day with a message from Dalat. Sau met him as he was going over the monkey bridge to Kar's village. Instantly, Sau knew that something was wrong.

"What is it?" he asked.

"I came to see you," the man said, obviously holding back bad news.

"Why?" Sau asked as the two of them bounced over the bridge toward Sim Jong.

The man waited until they had crossed and climbed the steep bank, then turned and spoke confidentially:

"You must come for a judgment."

"A judgment?" Sau asked. "Who is the accuser and who the accused."

"You are the accused," the messenger said. "The district chief at Dalat has sent for you."

Sau knew that this was not the work of his friend Loc.

"But why?" he demanded. The man still held back.

"You must answer to the charges of the people," the messenger said.

As they made their way along the brush-lined path from the river to the village, Sau pressed the man. Slowly, he drew from him the nature of the trouble he faced. Sau learned that the tribesmen who went back to the mountains had stirred up fury against him. Finding ready listeners among those who had never left, these grumblers said that Sau caused all the misery for the people at Thach Trai. Then they went to the government with their complaints, charging that Sau had deliberately taken their people out of the mountains to a land that was hot and disease-ridden and where no food would grow.

Sau, they advised the district chief, would cause the death of many tribesmen.

By persistently prodding the messenger, Sau further learned that besides the people's complaints, the district chief had an accusation of his own: Sau had taken away citizens of the district without the chief's consent.

But the most disturbing report was yet to be revealed. Somehow, Sau sensed his companion had more to say. He continued to coax the messenger into talking. Finally, the man said, dropping his voice to a whisper:

"I have not yet told you of the jungle men. They have already tried you. They found you guilty of taking the people to a place beyond their reach."

So that was it!

In his mind's eye Sau could see the clandestine court, a handful of black-clad men gathered around flaming torches. One or two would recount the grumblings they had picked up in the villages. Another would then remind them that Sau had already been marked for death. The leader—no doubt one whom Sau at some time had met in the path—would then pronounce sentence. Sau did not have to be told what it would be, but the messenger now spoke it:

"They have said"—he hesitated—"you must die . . . they will hack you to bits."

That night the moon shone brightly on the valley; at Sim Jong it silvered the thatched-roofs of a score or more houses.

The village slept—all but one man who prowled. Up and down he walked, like a noiseless, stalking tiger, between the straight rows of houses on the empty earthen street. The sandals he wore made a hushed, rhythmic sound. After a while, picking his way over tree roots and stones, he reached the log bridge that joined Jong Lo with Da Mham, and strode to the middle of the bridge. The swift-flowing water whispered in the moonlight and sang as it splashed beneath the place on which he stood.

He took note of the fact that the small chasm through which the river ran was capable of holding a great deal of water, so the villages were quite free from the threat of flooding.

But, he recalled, last rainy season the swollen river had covered the bridge, though with care the people still got across. The wet monsoon had started gently a year ago and the river rose slowly. He wondered if they shouldn't raise the bridge in anticipation of some sudden cloudburst.

But his thoughts were not long on the bridge or on the river. He faced a deluge in his soul, one that could overwhelm him. Sau was anguished by the hatred of his friends—his God-Follower friends.

He walked back to his village. The houses he passed, dark now, were filled with people who, like the ones who went back to the mountains, had turned against him. Oh, these had not called him vile names; none here had brought charges. But in their hearts, in their silence, he knew they too were bitter against him.

In the other villages of the valley it was the same. There were a few exceptions—the loyal Drim, his brother Kar and Kar's steadfast wife; the quiet, thoughtful Doi among the Roglai; maybe Sieng, who was God's man in the village at the far end of the bridge.

The others, though, were not only complaining against him, but were blaming God for their hardship.

"They don't say Sau has caused their sadness," one told him, "as much as they say God has forgotten them."

He recalled that day he had read about—the day in olden times when God would have given up His rebellious children had it not been for the eloquent plea of Moses. This great man had prayed for God to obliterate him instead of the people, and in Sau there was enough of a Moses to plead for these children here whose ways must be exasperating to God.

To pray, he now stopped his pacing and looked up at the sky. God, he knew, was there—the Spirit of the Skies—and Sau was not bound to the earth as the heathen were bound. He lifted his soul, confessing first, then asking that his heart be filled with the love of Jesus Christ.

"I have made mistakes," he said in his prayer. "I thought that to come to this valley would be to deliver my people from all their troubles. Here, I thought, they would find safety and abundance."

The valley had been a haven of safety from the jungle men, but that was as much as he could say. There was no abundance here; not even the yield of their old mountain slopes. Provision as well as safety rested with God. Yet, few among his people seemed to know that it was the Spirit of the Skies whom they had to trust.

"Where along the way have I let them lose their dependence on God?" he cried half aloud.

He tried to put from his mind the hatred that his people had for him. But he could not brush it away as one swept aside the annoying jungle flies. He could not forget. It would have been easy to become a prey to bitterness. Could he ever forgive?

He recalled what Grandfather and Grandmother had taught in the tribes center school, and how their lives portrayed what they taught. Once Grandmother told of Christ's admonition to Peter that he should forgive an enemy seventy times seven.

"This makes four hundred ninety times," she said with a mischievous glint in her eye. "Did Jesus mean not to forgive the four hundred ninety-first? Should one strike his tormentor after that?"

One student thought that after enduring four hundred ninety wrongs a person was justified in striking such a rascal.

But it now came to Sau that God had been wronged by everyone in this valley—seventy times seven was just a start—and still God was willing to forgive.

"Let God give *me* a heart of forgiveness," he prayed.

Bitterness, Sau knew, brought only sorrow to the bitter one. He prayed not only for his people's escape from a rankling spirit, but for his own release from theirs.

"Father God," he implored, "don't let them die from bitterness. And don't let my heart grow hard toward them."

K'Sol had taught him patience—this little man who, before God got hold of him, had run roughshod over anyone who happened to stand in his way. In front of Sau's eyes K'Sol had changed, and although he now suffered from a painful sickness K'Sol was still a patient, gentle man. Sau needed a world of patience; sensing that K'Sol's mantle had begun to slip from his shoulder, he asked that the portion of patience would fall on him.

But Sau faced a practical problem, too; a judgment hung over his head. By the grace of God he could forgive those who brought it; by the commands of men he had to go now and face it.

In the morning Sau made ready to leave for Dalat. He would walk the twisting road that threaded through swamps in its attempt to stay close to the river that ran to Nha Trang. In that city he would board a bus for the long climb to the pretty town up near the clouds. Before leaving, he went out to his field and tasted the soil once again. It was still good. He couldn't explain why it had chosen to be so miserly. He walked from the new hills of corn to his rice field. Dropping to one knee, he examined the grain closely. What he saw excited him.

"This will be good rice," he said. An image of his old smile returned to brighten his face. But promptly he grew grave again. He had voiced such optimistic thoughts before. Perhaps, in view of what lay ahead, he would never know whether this prophecy was right or wrong.

Sau went back to the house to say good-by to his wife and family. Each knew that meeting again was an uncertainty. If condemned by the government, his punishment would be severe. But beyond that stood a sentence already pronounced by the jungle men: Death by slow dismemberment.

Should he be freed by the government, the guerrillas had only to overtake him.

A few days after Sau's departure, Ha Rong's wife was carried out of the valley by the same road to the hospital in Nha Trang. Silently, grimly, Ha Rong watched her leave. She was going, he felt sure, to her death.

And when she had died, his children would go to another for raising. They would no longer be his. He would be alone, an old man before his time.

Impatiently, he turned to a pen where he kept some pigs. Lifting out one of them, he trussed the squealing swine by the spindled hind legs to a fence post, then with his knife slit the throat. The blood poured over Ha Rong's hands. Some of it he smeared on his forehead, some on the doorposts to his house.

"Spirits of the north and the south," he sang out with a fanatical ring to his voice, "bring health to the body of my wife!"

Then having completed his sacrifice to the demons, he set his angular face toward Heaven, looked over the roof of his house, and into the clouds.

"Did the Spirit of the Skies see the spilled blood of my pig?" He thrust a fist upward and shook it. "Did the God of Heaven hear me pray as of old to spirits of evil?"

A man who sat nearby in the doorway of his house certainly did. This neighbor both saw and heard Ha Rong's defiant act. And, feeling sick and hungry and lonesome for his mountains, the neighbor, only with difficulty, subdued the urge to join Ha Rong in his cursing.

12

Other People Come

SAU STOOD BEFORE THE DESK of the chief of Dalat's province. It was a big desk, nearly clear of papers, as tidy as the short, thick man with the military bearing who sat behind it. The room, too, was big and high ceilinged; two rows of smaller desks facing each other formed a center aisle from the corridor door.

Other neat men sat behind the desks, a corps of secretaries who waited for the chief to hand on a paper or give an order to the first secretary, whose desk was nearest. Then the first secretary would pass the paper or the order to the next, and so on down the line.

Sau, too, was dressed neatly. He wore the best suit he had, his burial suit. Under the circumstances, it did not seem inappropriate.

He felt the stares of the ten secretaries on his back. The chief was reading a document which the first secretary had placed in his hands; he knew that the document concerned him.

The district chief to whom the people complained had forwarded a presentment against Sau. This official, in passing his findings on to his superior, had added his own charge, contained in the report that the man whom Sau faced was now reading.

" . . . and this same tribesman Sau, on the date specified above, took his people beyond the boundary of the district. He did this without permission of the chief of district, the undersigned."

The provincial chief gathered up the papers and handed them to the first secretary, who paid little attention to them. Like his fellow secretaries, he found the spectacle of a tribesman on trial more entertaining than the handling of official papers.

The chief looked up to begin the interrogation Sau had been awaiting. At last he said loudly enough so that the clerks at the end of the room could hear without straining, "Your people say you took them to a hot climate."

Sau nodded. "They do not lie. To a tribesman from the mountains, the valley of Thach Trai would seem hot."

"They say they starved."

"This is also true. For some reason, the rice and corn did not grow well last season."

"Many fell sick," the officer continued.

"Many *were* sick," Sau admitted. "We prayed to the God of Heaven and more than a few are now better."

Sau tried to read his expression, but could not. The chief rose, walked briskly to the desk of the first secretary, and retrieved the papers containing the charges. He read again from the paper on top.

"You took your people out of the district without permission of the district chief." At this Sau heard the civil servants behind him clucking their disapproval.

"I meant no disobedience," Sau said. He had been standing, palms at his side, straight and stiff as a tree trunk. Now, he lowered his head and ran his finger around inside his collar to wipe away the sweat. This done, he felt better. Straightening again, he went on:

"I only wanted to take my people away from the jungle men"—at the mention of the words, a hush fell over the room—"to a safe place and to help them. I only meant to carry out in my own way what the government said we must do."

He looked straight ahead to the swivel chair which the chief had just vacated. Then he raised his eyes to a window behind the chair. Outside, beyond it, he saw a flowering plant that made him think of tasseled corn. He continued to stare at the plant. He pretended that it was corn, healthy corn, with big ears and big kernels on the big ears. He continued to stare, even when he sensed the chief had moved alongside him and now half-sat on the front of the desk and thrust his face close to Sau's. The big kernels then seemed to fade away and when they were gone Sau turned his head to look at the chief, who looked squarely at him.

"Did you always have food in the mountains?" the chief asked.

"No. Many times we went hungry," Sau replied.

"Did you have sickness before moving?"

"The mosquito found us there, too."

"Are you loyal to the government?"

Sau said he was loyal first to God, then to his country. Yes, he felt that he could say he was loyal.

The chief walked once more to the secretary's desk, threw down the papers, then crossed behind his own desk to the window. He turned his back to the room, and stood there looking out. All were aware that in the decision he was now making, rested a tribesman's fate. But the chief's stance told them nothing. To Sau the loud ticking of the clock on the wall sounded like his own heartbeat, magnified many times. A telephone in an outer office rang and rang unnervingly. No one answered. Within the room the silence was heavy. Sau could not take his eyes from the back of the chief's thick neck.

After what seemed aeons, the chief turned and walked back to the first secretary's desk.

"Write out for this man an order of acquittal," he said. "I will be pleased to sign it."

With a few words he dismissed Sau, who bobbed his head politely, his face now glowing with astonished gratitude. As Sau turned to go down the aisle of desks to the door, past the stony-faced secretaries who had not recovered from their amazement at seeing an accused tribesman walk out free, the chief said to the first secretary, and again the most distant clerk could hear, "I wish I had that man on my staff."

Sau stepped out into the sunlight. He looked about him uneasily. One sentence of death had been lifted. But another was still in force. He was free, and yet he wasn't free. He was still a condemned man; let him fall into the hands of the guerrillas, who seemed able to turn up anywhere at any time, and his fate was certain.

There was another judgment, too, against him, and this was the one that made him feel sad. It was the feeling of his own people in the valley. Could he ever go back now? Would they accept him once more as their pastor?

Fortunately, he did not have to face this situation at once. He stayed for a while in Dalat to tend to his duties, as he was still an official in the church. This was 1959; the government of Viet Nam had just accorded citizenship to the tribespeople. For this reason the Christian and Missionary Alliance felt that the churches of the tribes and the Vietnamese should be joined, and took steps to encourage this.

The day came when Sau had to return to his village.

Sau decided to travel over the same route by which he had left.

He would ride the bus to Nha Trang; then he would set out on foot. During the long ride he was reminded of the dark uncertainties that lay ahead when he had come this way to Dalat. But none of the threats had materialized. Now he was absolved of every charge—God had intervened, he felt—and he was going home. His heart should have been light. Yet uncertainties of a different kind loomed ahead. What kind of home-coming would he find? Would he ever *reach* his village?

Perhaps the Viet Cong might have kept watch on his movements. On the crowded bus from Dalat he peered at the faces around him. He looked for cold, glinting eyes that might betray the intent of a killer. He found none. The bus was not stopped at a Viet Cong road-block and searched for marked men, as sometimes happened. In walking the lonely road that led from the coast to the valley, he con-stantly scanned the fringes of the jungle for movement of a lurking enemy.

But here he was nearing home, and the closer he got the less he thought of attack and the more of his wife Drim and of conditions in the five villages. He wondered if the people were still hungry, and still spiritually starved, and sick. Coming on Da Mham, which was the first of the villages to be reached from the road, he broke into a run, so anxious was he to get home.

He saw nothing unusual in this village, no obvious answers to his questions. He decided to skirt it and hurry on to his own village. He quickly crossed the log bridge to Jong Lo. As he did he he darted his eyes in every direction for a sign.

He found one—he thought it was an indication—as he drew in sight of his house. He saw his old mother-in-law treading the short stalks of unflailed rice, the loose-hanging lobes of her ears flopping in rhythm to the stamp of her bare feet. Close by, he saw Drim husk-ing the rice by pounding it in a mortar and winnowing it in the slight breeze.

There had been at least some harvest!

The meat of a buffalo and the carcass of a goat hung side-by-side on a line to dry in the sun. In the brown roof of the church he saw bright green patches; someone had kept the thatch in repair.

Sau advanced silently, grinning broadly, full of hope, yet not quite sure. He called to his wife. She turned.

"Minoi!" she cried.

Throwing down her pounding pole, she ran to him. She buried her face in her arms.

"You're home!"

"I'm free!"

"Those awful charges—" She looked up, uncertain.

"I'm free," he repeated. Drim wept as he recounted the story of his acquittal. When he had finished, she looked at her husband searchingly.

"But the other . . . that condemnation by the jungle men—"

"I'm here, am I not?" he said smiling. He squeezed her hand to reassure her.

"But you are not safe," she said, her voice husky with concern.

"The guerrillas," he said. "Why did they not try to kill me there?" Drim was not satisfied.

"They know Dalat has many soldiers." she replied.

"Why did they not stop the bus, then, if they wanted me? Why did they not lie in ambush for me as I walked the road all alone by the river?"

His questions made her worries sound unreasonable. She had no answers. And yet—her heart beat fast with fear for his life.

"I have heard how vicious tribesmen slip under the house of an enemy at night and drive a spear through the floor and into his kidney," she said. "Cannot the jungle men do the same to one they have marked for death?"

"There are no jungle men about," he said. He drew her toward where old Duin was still trampling the stalks with her feet.

"Doubly old mother!" he called, greeting her with much respect. "You seem to have a big stack of rice to thresh. Tell me—tell me—just how big?"

The news that Sau was back spread rapidly in all the villages. The people were happy to see him. Sau could have cried. It was so different from the home-coming against which he had braced himself. As they crowded into his house to welcome him back, none seemed to remember they had been offended because of him. He hardly remembered it himself.

Why was everyone in such high spirits?

First one then another invited him to their homes to sit down at the table with them.

"I want you to eat my rice," a man of Kar's village said.

"You ought to taste my new corn and squash," said one of his own people, a Chil.

After several such invitations Sau began to understand. Perhaps some were trying to express their remorse for the thought they had held against him; but of this he wasn't sure. What he could clearly see was that all wanted to show off to him the fruits of a bountiful harvest!

Sau asked questions about their crops. They beamed as they described it: rice, corn, manioc, fruits of many kinds. No one had ever seen such abundance!

"My storehouse is crammed," said one. "The grain overflows into the house I live in."

"We eat and eat and we have food left over," added another. "Even the dogs are getting fat."

"And a new crop is well on the way," said still another.

There had been good fishing, too, and in the forest good hunting— deer, wild pig, and peacock.

No longer did they complain of the heat. The sickness seemed to be gone.

"Our fevers have stopped," said Sieng, the pastor in Da Mham. "And our stomachs don't pain us any more as they once did."

Only one village had lagged behind the others—Da Mur. The people in this farthest settlement had enough to eat, but it was not all of their own effort.

"We help them, but we help a lazy people who won't even remove the stones from their fields," said their neighbors, the Tring and the Chil.

Sau was especially concerned over Ha Rong.

"He used to like the people and they liked him," one who had known Ha Rong a long time said. "Now he spends much time alone, brooding in his house or out by himself in the forest."

Not long after his return, Sau crossed over the swaying monkey bridge to pay a visit to Da Mur.

On his way he noted that the bridge had been improved. It had withstood the high, swift waters of the last rainy season. The work the people had done on the bridge and on their homes and churches impressed Sau. But it also made him cautious. He hoped this new enthusiasm—which extended to things spiritual—did not depend on just the fortune of their fields.

What they had experienced was God's goodness—no question—he said to himself. But it was easy to forget to love the giver, in loving the gift.

Reaching Da Mur, he stopped first at Ha Rong's. He had heard the astounding news that Ha Rong's wife returned from the hospital and that the prayers of believers had healed her. Greeting her, he spoke of God's goodness.

The woman said nothing. He asked if any but God had healed her. Still she remained silent in her darkened house.

How strange, he thought, for one whose life had been spared to refuse to say that God spared it. He asked where Ha Rong was.

"He is away," she said abruptly.

"Where did he go?"

"He went to the forest."

"Why is he in the forest?"

She hesitated, turning aside to poke the fire in the clay box. "He's looking for roots and leaves to eat. We cannot eat the rocks that lie in our sandy soil."

This was the one cloud in the valley's bright sky—the continued bitterness of Ha Rong. He was still one who would rather complain than remedy his discomfort.

But soon Sau had a greater sadness. He heard one day that K'Sol had died. K'Sol, the little man who had picked Sau out of the market so many years before and showed him how one truly became a follower of the God of Heaven; K'Sol, who had urged Sau to learn new things, who had taught him to do what the Bible said and to lead his people in obedience to God's commands—beloved K'Sol, of whom there would never be another, was gone, and for days Sau felt that a part of his own soul had been lowered into the grave.

His sadness was tempered, however, as he thought back to those days with K'Sol, at the tribes center when it was only a one-room slab-sided shack, and on evangelistic missions in the pagan villages. K'Sol had drawn pictures of Heaven on an easel while he talked. Now he would know if his pictures were true.

Now K'Sol would know that Heaven was better than Charnier's glittering store in Saigon.

But Sau and the others who loved K'Sol had little time for mourning. The trails into the valleys were resounding to the tramp of tribesmen's feet. New people were coming to Thach Trai! Word of the

valley's harvest had reached them. They wanted to share the fruits of
so bountiful a land.

Many of those who came by the hundreds were spirit worshipers
from the mountains, who had once feared Thach Trai as the dwelling
place of demons. But the God-Followers, it now seemed to them, had
broken the spell. These who had once vowed mass suicide by poison
rather than leave the land of their ancestors now came willingly,
eagerly. Even old grannies forgot their obligations to the graves of
the ancestors and the gods of the mountains.

Life flourished at Thach Trai.

Their coming gave the God-Followers a job to do. The new villages springing up around them became fertile fields in which to plant
the Gospel seed.

Young people, especially those led by Kar and Doi, visited the new
pagan villages in order to preach and teach. They invited the newcomers, most of whom were Roglai, to enormous feasts. The pagans
went home laden with baskets of meat and rice, gifts from hosts glad
to have had them come. Along with the baskets of food, they took
with them the impression that here in this valley had come a people
who now lived in peace and real joy.

Bountiful harvests became the rule—twice a year for some crops,
three times for others. In food supply, in health, in opportunities
for spiritual witness, in contentment, these children of God had never,
since birth, known such a good life. Even Ha Rong occasionally
seemed to have turned from his backsliding and bitterness and to be
his old self.

What more could life offer? To live happily and comfortably, and
then someday the easy journey to Heaven. . . . Had Eden been re-
created?

But one day—toward the end of summer in 1960—a man returning from his field to Da Mur saw two strangers ahead in the path.
Neither was a tribesman, but Vietnamese, or so he thought; long, un-
kempt hair obscured race and nationality. They wore black collarless
shirts and black trousers cut off above the knee. Large knives hung
from their belts. On their feet were heavy boots, such as the ones the
Vietnamese army got from America—and which were considered a
prize in the spoils of guerrilla warfare.

The man of Da Mur greeted them: *"Niam sa?*—Is your body
good?" The strangers did not reply, seeming not to comprehend.

Plainly, they were not tribesmen. Instead, they pushed their stomachs in with their hands and pointed to their mouths to show that they were hungry.

The villager tried to make them understand that they were welcome to come home with him and sit at his table.

The two shook their heads. They indicated that they wanted the villager to bring them bowls of rice so they might eat there in the forest. But the man's sense of hospitality was strong; he beckoned them to follow him to his house, which they did.

The strangers ate as though they had been starved. When they finished, they strolled about the village. Their eyes grew wide as they observed the baskets of rice and the stacks of corn and squash in front of so many houses. They expressed their gratitude and indicated they would like to return for another meal the next day.

Their host nodded his acquiescence.

"God has given us our rice," he said. "We cannot refuse to share it."

On the following day the two men returned with a third. The newcomer was taller and heavier. He also wore a hat, an olive green jungle helmet. From his bearing, the villagers knew that he was the leader.

Unlike his silent companions he talked freely, partly in Vietnamese, partly in a poor effort in the tribal tongue; now the villagers knew he led the other two. All three were surprised when the tribesmen replied in Vietnamese. Believing their own language would fall on deaf ears, the visitors had not attempted any conversation. The leader, however, made more of an effort to ingratiate himself. He smiled and waved at the children who peered shyly out from doors and windows. He stopped at Ha Rong's pigsty to remark on the good fat swine. Ha Rong was away just now, but others could be counted on to pass along the compliment. He stepped inside the church, removed his helmet, and observed that the people must be very industrious to have erected such a fine edifice.

They were served a special meal of chopped chicken and fish mixed with vegetables. When they had finished, the man in the helmet belched noisily to show his enjoyment. Then he turned and spoke to the villagers who crowded around.

"We appreciate your favors," he said. "And soon we will repay them—when we have driven from the land the enemies of our people."

His voice rang as he said this. Then his tone became almost cajoling.

"Before we go, we have one more favor to ask."

An apprehensive hush descended on the villagers, who wondered what was coming next. They'd heard stories of the jungle men's demands from other tribesmen.

The leader took a few swift steps and picked up from the ground a section of bamboo. Whipping his knife from his belt, he swiftly and skillfully whittled one end to a needle-sharp point.

"Make us spears like this one," he urged. "Spears of bamboo."

His voice was still soothing. But in it now there was a note of command.

Another silence.

"How many do you want us to make?"

"As many as you have ears of corn from your fields."

Still no one said they would.

"It is in your own interest," he explained. "The spears will be used for your own protection."

"What protection do we need?" asked a man who was perhaps bolder than the rest.

"What protection?" The visitor's inflection indicated his surprise, as if this was something that they all ought to know. "Why, you need to be protected from the soldiers along the seacoast who will ride up the road in their trucks and point their guns in your faces and take away your fine villages and fields."

His smile disappeared, like the sun behind a cloud. He said sternly, "To stop them you must make the pointed spears, then plant them thickly in the road between your valley and the coast. We will show you how—and where."

He stopped to let the command sink in. After a moment the bolder one asked:

"Do you mean we should plant them as we once planted spears on the graves of our dead to keep away the evil spirits?"

"That is right," the leader said with a nod. He picked up his helmet in readiness to leave. "Plant them in the road as if it were a grave."

With a gesture to the others, he strode away, in apparent confidence that the spears would be made.

13

A Date Remembered

ONE DAY the people of Thach Trai awoke to find the guerrillas had moved into the mountains. They now surrounded the valley on three sides. And, the villagers quickly discovered, the highway to the coast was closed.

They were in real danger. One of them, a man named Mang, had tried to walk to Nha Trang on the coast to trade mushrooms for salt. He had gone about two thirds of the way when he found bamboo spikes across the road.

Some of the sharp points, he noticed, were thick with a dark brown substance, which he recognized as the deadly poison of the Roglai.

Mang looked about him. Wide stretches of impenetrable swamp lay on either side of the road as far as he could see. He could go no farther. Wait a minute! There was one way, one last route left open to him and to any fellow villagers who wanted to go to the coast: the river.

For years the Roglai had been accustomed to using rafts to go down to Nha Trang to work off their taxes. From them the Chil and the Tring learned to use rafts too, although these tribes were less skillful, and they were afraid of the water because they were not good swimmers.

Mang hurriedly returned to Da Mham with his news, which soon spread to all the villages. Excitedly, the people talked of how the guerrillas persuaded those in the nearby pagan villages to make bamboo spikes and plant them in the road.

Later, as the villagers continued the discussions around their cooking fires, some said their situation was not so bad. Why should they have to go out, after all? Food was plentiful; the biggest harvest yet was coming along in their fields. Their houses were comfortable. The churches were in good repair. They were no longer afflicted by sick-

175

ness. They could get by in isolation for a long while. But others pointed out that they were overlooking the threat of the jungle men.

Among those who held this viewpoint was Sau.

"They will return," he warned. "Next time, many more than three will come."

Sau had the wholehearted support of two men with influence in the village. Their names were Gai and Jieng.

Gai was Loc's representative for all the settlements of the valley. He carried on his work from a government house that had been erected in Da Mham. Gai was rather squat, with a head that seemed too big for his body—except that having eaten amply at Thach Trai he now had a stomach to match. He was a likeable fellow, firm but not unkind in his manner, one who spoke with clarity. He filled his official role well.

Jieng was tall and thin. He was a soldier who trained the young men of the villages as a home guard. They were hardly a formidable army. Their only weapons were shoulder axes and knives. Nevertheless, Jieng took his duties seriously. The two men differed in one important respect: Jieng asked his pastor to pray that God would help him carry out his tasks; Gai did not.

"We may not have much time to save ourselves from the jungle men," said Gai. "We ought to be building fences around our villages right now, and perhaps planting bamboo spikes outside the fences."

Early one morning—it was October 15, and he would remember the date well—Sau knelt in the corner of his house and prayed, "Let God make us stand firm and strong like a good house post that does not rot."

Later that day he walked briskly from Jong Lo to Kar's village. He felt he must speak at once with his brother. He found Kar working at the church. The two sat down on a bench and looked at the houses that stretched away on either hand. They were conscious of the danger that was uppermost in both their minds. But for a time, as they talked of this and that, neither mentioned it. Sau brought up the subject first.

"We must be ready," he said. "We cannot know when to expect them, or in what spirit they will come."

Kar turned and look apprehensively.

"Is it you that they are after?" he asked.

Sau was silent a moment.

"No, I don't think so," he replied. "If they had wanted to kill me, they would not have shown themselves beforehand." The lines of worry in his face grew deeper. "I'm concerned about our people. We know uncertain days are ahead. Will they be strong enough to meet them?"

" 'God is our refuge and strength,' " said Kar, quoting from one of his favorite Psalms.

"We must read God's Word every day. The strength of God comes from the Word of God," Sau went on. "But here is our problem. The old people cannot read. The young ones we have taught to read, but many times they do not. Because of this there is only one answer. The people of each village must gather in their churches every evening, after the work is done."

Kar nodded.

"We can sing the hymns we know," he said. "We can spend time in prayer. Every pastor can read and explain those parts of God's Word that are written in our tongue."

Now Sau nodded his approval.

"We must meet God in God's house every single day," he said emphatically. "We do not know when trouble will strike."

Kar jumped to his feet. "My people will gather here this night. And I will invite the villagers of Da Mur to come across the river to join us."

Kar started across the river that same afternoon to extend his invitation. At the far end of the monkey bridge he met a boy who had been running. The lad's eyes were wide, his face contorted with fear, as he tried to convey his message.

"They've come again!" he blurted.

Kar did not have to ask who had come.

"Poh, our pastor, is sick at Jong Lo," the boy went on. "My mother sent me to get you."

Kar continued on his way toward Da Mur, this time on a dead run.

The three dreaded visitors had announced their return by a thunderous shout. Most of the women were boiling the evening's rice over their clay fireboxes. The men were resting, having just come in from the fields. Only a few children were about.

"Come out of your houses!" a voice called in their own dialect, and the command went echoing down the street. The children shrieked and ran for cover; women dropped their spoons; bare feet bounded from beds to the springy floors; all over the village eyes peered cautiously through slits in the bamboo walls or warily around corners.

Those who looked saw the husky leader and his two confederates stride to the church and take up a stand before it. The tall one had dispensed with the surface geniality of his previous visit. He now stood coldly, his arms folded across his collarless, sleeveless black shirt, waiting impassively for them to gather. The villagers had a feeling they ought not to be too long about it.

As they assembled before him they thought he seemed more determined than angry, as though he would brook no denial of any request he might make. A few, in fact, thought his stance and his olive helmet combined to give him a certain dignity.

When he was satisfied that they had all gathered—or nearly all— he spoke: "We have come for the spikes." There was silence. No one stirred. No one answered. "The spikes—the ones you were to make for us," he went on evenly and without emotion. The crowd, which now numbered nearly two hundred, was quiet; a few turned their heads away, avoiding his gaze.

"Where are those spikes?" the leader asked. He spoke in his native Vietnamese, occasionally repeating a word in their tongue to make sure they understood. When this question received no answer, a faint smile crossed his lips. But it vanished in a moment. When he spoke again it seemed as though he hadn't really smiled.

"Where do you keep them?" he asked, still without raising his voice.

Again no answer.

"Come now, do you mean to say that you have made none?" An incredulous irony marked his tone.

A long silence, this time a painful one. Then a voice, indistinguishable among the villagers, called out:

"You are right! We have made none!"

The leader replied with strained patience above the rising murmurs:

"You do not seem to understand what we ask, or why we ask it. Others have made spikes, and we have put them to good use."

"We know what you're up to," shouted the one who had called out before. He was in the thick of the crowd, and because he was rather short he dared to be bold—so long as the visitors could not see him. Even so, he crouched a little as he shouted again. "You are using the spikes to block the road! You want to hold us captives in this valley!"

The guerrilla leader exhibited a look of hurt surprise.

"We are your friends," he said in a tone of conciliation. Quickly, he jerked open his shirt to show that he wore no weapon except a knife of the kind carried by everyone who walked the jungle trails. But in a sudden shift of mood he again sounded as though he were issuing a command as he went on to say:

"We want you people to come with us to the mountains. Not just the young men. All of you."

A murmur of dismay ran through the crowd.

"We cannot go," someone shouted—not the crouching man in the middle, but another who hoped he would not be recognized.

"Why not?" the leader inquired evenly.

"Our pastor is sick. He cannot take us."

"Your pastor belongs to yesterday," the guerrilla leader replied, his eyes deadly cold. "You do not need him. We will show you the way to tomorrow. We will teach you things your pastor never learned."

The opposition of the crowd was growing firmer. There were a few, however, who were intrigued and wanted to hear more.

"Tell us what you would teach us!" an old woman demanded. Before the guerrilla could reply, there was a commotion at the edge of the crowd. Gai had arrived at the scene.

"Here is Gai," a man called out above the burst of nervous chatter. "He is our government man. He knows about these things. What does he say?"

Others repeated the question. Gai leaped up on a stump. Taking one look at the garb of the man who was addressing this gathering, he said tersely, "Don't listen to him. Pay no attention to anything he says," and jumped down.

There was another stir at the edge of the crowd. A newcomer, somewhat taller than the others, was making his way through the throng in the direction of the guerrilla leader.

"It's Pastor Kar from Sim Jong!" a voice cried out. "He'll tell us what to do. Yes, hear what Pastor Kar says!"

Paying no attention to the guerrilla, Kar took his place beside him and faced the crowd. Although slighter than the jungle man, he was his equal in height. The villagers of Da Mur were quiet, waiting for his words.

"Do you remember what my brother Sau said to you?" Kar asked. " 'Have nothing to do with these men,' that's what he said. He warned you because they are jungle men, just like the ones who gave us trouble when we lived back in the mountains."

Kar noticed from the corner of his eye that his words made no visible impression on the guerrilla leader. But how about the people who stood before him?

Of all the God-Followers in the valley, Kar knew these Tring, with a few exceptions, were the weakest in spirit. Their land here was the poorest and they had done little to help themselves. It was difficult for them to drop the superstitions that had bound them. He did not know whether they would listen, but he decided to plead with them once more:

"Don't make the bamboo spikes! Above all, don't go to the forest with them! They're trying to trick you. Once you are in the jungle, you will be in their power. Come over the monkey bridge to the house of God in my village tonight. My brother Sau will be there. Sau will tell you God's Word."

He said no more.

But the people turned away, and by their turning gave the stranger his answer. This was their refusal to go to the mountains with him, their refusal to make the bamboo spikes. The leader, glowering now, was left with his two companions. They stood for a moment, speaking together in whispers. Then they gradually edged past the houses and toward the forest. They had scarcely left the clearing when one of the villagers broke from the knot of stragglers and ran after them.

It was Ha Rong.

He did not return until dark. Then he crossed to a small house next to the church and mounted the veranda by a notched pole.

Inside the house a man sat at a small table reading his hymnal by the light of a homemade candle. Ha Rong called to him softly:

"Uncle, come out. I want to speak to you."

Startled, the man laid the book down on the table and walked out onto the veranda.

"Why did you call me?" he asked irritably. The whole village was on edge; and to be summoned into the night after such a day was enough to disturb any man.

"I am afraid," said Ha Rong.

"Are we not all afraid?" the older man replied. "Would we not all be on our way to hear the teaching of Pastor Sau in Sim Jong if we dared walk the path?"

"I fear the jungle men will come back tonight," said Ha Rong. "I am especially afraid for you."

"Why me?" the older man asked.

"I am afraid for you because you hold the tithe for the church of our village," Ha Rong said. "The strangers know that. They will come back to take it from you."

"If they know it," said the man, the church treasurer, "it is because you have told them." An exclamation burst from his lips. "Who has not seen you going into the forest?"

"Yes, I have gone into the forest," Ha Rong admitted readily, appearing to be hurt by the remark, "and I have talked with the jungle men. But I have done this only to learn what they intend to do."

For a moment the two remained silent; the night noises of the frogs and the insects could be heard coming from the jungle. Ha Rong spoke again:

"How much does the tithe amount to?"

"More than any man in the village possesses," the treasurer replied.

"How much?" Ha Rong insisted.

The treasurer compressed his lips. Then with a sigh he uttered the words.

"More than a thousand piasters."

He hadn't wanted to say it, but it was hard to hold out against Ha Rong, who was as persistent as he was persuasive.

"Of course you have buried it in a place of safekeeping," Ha Rong said casually.

"No, I have not buried it."

"It lies in your house?" Ha Rong's voice rose in alarm.

The treasurer was offended. He did not like to be thought careless with God's money.

"Indeed it does not lie in my house," he replied curtly. "I have it here in the pocket of my trousers." He patted a lump on his hip.

Ha Rong moved closer to the doorway and squatted on the veranda. The treasurer stooped beside him.

Again they fell silent. But Ha Rong had not finished.

"I fear for your life," he resumed. "And I fear for what will happen to the money of our church when you are dead."

"When I'm dead—" The treasurer gasped. To him, responsibility for the tithe was a sacred trust. He had often wondered if he might one day be required to honor it with his life. But afterward? It had never occurred to him what would happen to the money after he died.

"What can I do?" he asked, thoroughly shaken.

"I don't know," Ha Rong answered with finality.

"Shall I bury it?"

Ha Rong shrugged. "The fresh digging would reveal the hiding place."

"I have no place to conceal it in my house." His voice trembled, his body shook.

"You could give it to another," Ha Rong suggested, as if suddenly struck by a new thought. "If someone carried it in his pocket, the jungle men would not know where to seek it."

That was a promising idea. The treasurer sighed deeply.

"But who—"

"I will take it," Ha Rong volunteered quickly. "It would never occur to the jungle men that *I* have the church's tithe."

The treasurer agreed. Then he hesitated. He remembered that Ha Rong hardly ever came to church any more. Hadn't all the villagers heard the rumors of his return to sacrificing? If true, he would not let that pagan touch God's money. Still, there was no one else. He was undoubtedly the one with whom the money would be safest.

The treasurer stood up, reached into his pocket and took out a thick fold of large soiled piaster notes, in different colors, some purple, some rose, some blue. Looking longingly at the roll, he said:

"The price of a water buffalo is here. Also the price of food that people denied themselves. I myself gave a tithe from my crop when I needed all of it. Never mind, someday it will buy a metal roof for the house of God. Here—take good care of it."

He thrust the money at Ha Rong, who slipped it into his pocket. Then Ha Rong said he had a new inspiration. He would bury the money in the forest.

"Come with me and watch me hide it," he urged.

The treasurer shook his head. Ha Rong might have reverted to paganism, but he had no reason not to trust him in money matters. Anyway, he had already made the decision to put the money in Ha Rong's care.

"No," the treasurer replied. "I wish to read more of my hymnal before my candle is gone." He went back into the house.

Letting himself down the notched pole, Ha Rong hurried to the path that led into the jungle.

In a few minutes a dozen guerrillas swept from the forest into Da Mur. They were an ill-assorted group. Some wore black calico, some parts of army uniforms. Some were armed with automatic guns or carbines, some with small weapons.

All obeyed the sharply barked commands of the leader who had addressed the village in the afternoon.

Once again he took up his stand in front of the church. This time, when the villagers were slow to assemble, he made no effort to conceal his impatience.

"Hurry them up! Get them all out here!" he bawled to his men. "Go into their houses and bring them out. Bring a light! Bring firebrands! Bring an oil lamp! The pastor's house has one, I know."

Children screamed and old people cried out, their sounds mingling with the orders of the fanatical invaders. In the confusion the villagers were rounded up, herded into a tight knot, and made to stand before the Viet Cong leader.

Several torches soon lighted the scene. By the glow of the flares and the pastor's lamp, which someone brought out, the people could see they were ringed by gunmen; there could be no escaping the closed circle. They were frozen by the wild nightmare in which they were taking part.

The church treasurer stood near the outer edge of the crowd. He was congratulating himself for having placed the tithe money in safekeeping when a familiar figure, brandishing a carbine, moved into view.

Ha Rong?

He swung his head around for a second look. In the light of a flare he saw the taut cords of the long thin neck. A look of embarrassment crossed the lean face. It was Ha Rong! As the treasurer called out, Ha Rong turned away. He could not bear to confront one whom he so recently had defrauded.

Tears filled the treasurer's eyes. How neatly he had been duped! He realized that Ha Rong must have been one of the jungle men for a long time. He recalled the suspicions, the murmurings of others. He now heard the gasps of dismay from those who also were seeing Ha Rong for what he really was.

Oh, Ha Rong was persuasive, all right! He knew he had to get his hands on the money before the raid, and he let nothing stand in his way. He knew that the treasurer, rather than give it up to an enemy, would have fed it to his goat.

The treasurer looked closely to see if the crafty one's pocket still bulged with the roll. It did not. But he did see what might have been a fattened pocket on the hip of the husky leader.

"We come to teach you people," the rebel chief snarled at the villagers. There was not even self-control this time, no show of studied patience. In the weird light of the flares his eyes flamed like a tiger's.

"If you will not learn one way, you must learn another," he declared. "You will learn that we are right and the government is wrong. They've sold you to America, just as once you were sold to France. But America is dying. Dying! Do you hear? We are the party of Ho Chi Minh. He will drive America from Asia—he will bring your God to His knees!"

The treasurer hardly heard the outburst. The face of Ha Rong, now turned back toward him and suddenly hardened with hatred, claimed his attention. Of those who trained guns on the shivering villagers, Ha Rong seemed to wear the most sinister expression.

He was a man whom they of the Tring had known all their lives, one who in spite of his waverings they had liked. He had been down, he had been up; first a pagan, then a deacon, and then a cursing sacrificer. But Ha Rong in all his previous aberrations had never reached the depths to which tonight he had descended.

Ha Rong was not alone in forsaking the group, or turning from the God of Heaven. Sitting by herself, apart from the villagers, was his wife. She, whom they once thought all but dead, and who was then raised by prayers of faith—she, too, had cast her lot with the enemy.

The guerrilla leader ranted on, condemning the government, the pastors of the villages, and God. As he talked a light rain began to fall. It resembled the gentle rain that started the wet monsoon, although that season was yet two months away. Alarmed lest their thatched houses be put to the torch, the villagers prayed for a downpour.

The guerrillas talked freely of their plans. They intended to move the people away. Then perhaps they would come back to loot the houses of food and things of value. Perhaps after that they would employ the torch. Here they would work out the master plan, which they would apply to all the villages.

When the villagers heard that all were to be led away deep into the dark jungle, an agonized shriek pierced the night.

"We won't go!" an old man shouted defiantly. "We won't go! We won't—" The blow of a gun butt cut short his protest.

"You *will* go," the guerrilla chief rejoined. "You will go and you will stay until your minds have been washed clean of the foolishness that now fills them.

"When you come back you will come as missionaries—missionaries for the Viet Cong—to teach others the new truths that you have been taught."

Nearly every woman was sobbing. But weeping was not confined to women.

"Our precious church!" a man cried. Yes, now that they were being taken away, now that they could not gather there mornings and nights to pray, as few had been doing in recent days, it indeed became precious.

"My hymnal is in my house," the treasurer said. He pleaded with Ha Rong that he be allowed to get it. But the group was already being moved like a large herd of water buffalo. Ha Rong, prodding them from behind, threatened to kill any who did not keep up.

"Where will these scared ones run to?" asked a tribesman from outside the valley who had joined the guerrillas. He laughed darkly. "Over a field of poisoned spears?"

Obedient by nature, cowed by the display of guns, the people of Da Mur fell into a manageable file for the trek through the forest to an unknown destination. There an ominous future awaited them.

In spite of the guns, however, about forty persons escaped in the dark. Some found their way to the bridge that crossed to Sim Jong. They ran at once to the church; there Sau had just finished teaching the evening lesson.

"Our people have been taken away!" they shouted. "The jungle men have come!"

The service broke up in confusion.

Sau managed to calm one of those who had escaped, but learned little more from him.

"They came with their guns and marched us away! I got free . . . and maybe my wife did. My son is gone."

Sau sought to instill some sort of order into the frenzied mob. At last he was able to do so, and he knelt to pray. But at that moment another man arrived. Panting breathlessly, he stammered out his warning.

"I heard them talking," he said. "They intend to kill you!"

"You have a gun," someone in the church cried out. "Get it."

It was true; Sau did have a gun. His friend Loc, the district chief at Nha Trang, had once given him an old one to use against the wild pigs that rooted in their cornfields.

"Get it out!" a voice cried again.

"Yes!" chorused others.

"It is our only protection," someone was heard to shout above the clamor. "If you don't, we'll all be killed."

The news quickly reached the other villages. People everywhere waited numbly for the jungle men to ravage their villages as they had ravaged Da Mur. In Da Mham, directly across the river from Jong Lo, fear had driven most of the people to huddle in darkened homes. Here the houses were not set up on stilts as in other villages; they sat on the ground, which made them especially vulnerable to attack.

Da Mham was on the same side of the river as Da Mur; the only barrier between it and the guerrillas was a small stream, and this could be forded without much difficulty. Living no more than a twenty-minute walk away, the people of Da Mham had reason to fear they might be next.

Sieng was pastor here. A ripened counselor for one not long past his teens, he forced himself to be calm as he talked with Gai, the government representative, and a man named Mang. The three sat in Gai's house, around a table beneath a hanging oil lamp. Mang advised Gai to flee.

"As the government's man, you will be the target of the guerrillas' fury," he said.

"Perhaps the people will flee with me." Gai was unsure, but hopeful.

"No," said Sieng. "We are too many. We could never escape. And if we ran, where would we run to? Into the arms of the jungle men who no doubt surround all the villages."

Just then Sieng's eyes were drawn to the open window. As he looked up he heard a click. He saw that from the window the barrel of a shotgun leveled at them. The click had been the hitting of hammer on pin!

The face behind the gun froze with astonishment. The gunman had fired to kill, hoping his shot would fell all three in the room, but there was no blast.

The three sprang to their feet. Instantly, faces appeared at all the windows and black-clad men crowded the doorway. From every side guns were trained on the center of the room. One aimed a revolver and squeezed on the trigger. This time there was not even a click; the gun had jammed.

The tall, bristling chief pushed past his men into the room to confront the three tribesmen. Earlier in the day Gai had seen him sullen but composed; now he was enraged. A submachine gun was slung from a shoulder, a pistol tucked in his belt. With muddied boots he kicked a bench out of his way.

"You chose the side of those who talk of God?" he spat at Gai. "You are doomed. Your God is doomed!"

His oaths were long and loud, but they trailed off. Then he spoke not just to Gai, but to all three motionless figures before him. "One day we will win. When we do we will feed the people well. But not you dogs—" He lifted the submachine gun to point in turn at each of the three. "You will be dead before that day."

He berated Gai for serving a government of monsters. Then he asked who was the pastor; Sieng said he was. The leader turned on Sieng, mocking him, calling him a bloodsucker that extorted the people's wealth and gave nothing in return.

He stalked back and forth in the room. Once he turned sharply and shouted:

"Lie on the floor!"

Sieng looked at Gai, and Gai at Mang. Each knew that to lie down was to be beaten with a gun butt or kicked and stomped by muddy feet. Quickly and silently among themselves they reached the decision to disobey.

"We will stand," Sieng said quietly.

"As you please," the chief said. Slowly and deliberately he drew the pistol from his waist.

"Wait!" a rebel in the doorway called out. "Twice we tried shooting, but our guns would not shoot."

"Bring a cord, then," the chief said, the man's words having strangely subdued him. With kicks he pushed the three tribesmen toward the door.

Outside, the rain had stopped, but the hardpacked earth before the house was slippery with mud. The night was pitch black until someone carried out the lamp from the house. From another quarter someone pushed a fourth man into the small ring of prisoners.

"He's Jieng," the captor explained to the chief. "He keeps the spears of the government house."

Someone else brought a rope. Jieng, with Gai and Mang, was trussed up and marched off to the forest. The chief pushed Sieng away, sending him sprawling in the mud. "We don't want him. He talks too much about the God of Heaven."

But Sieng struggled to his feet and tried to run after the departing band.

"I am their pastor! You must let me go with them," he shouted.

Again the chief pushed him aside. There would be another time, another way, to deal with preachers.

"We don't want him," he said again.

Many pairs of arms pushed Sieng into the mud and heavy boots kicked at him. He lay there in the darkness which grew darker still as the lamp moved with captors and captives away from the village common, beyond the church, and out of sight.

As he lay there, stunned and helpless, the final words of the guerrilla leader rang in his head:

"Pray for them if you wish. But pray fast. You don't have much time, you know."

In the Sim Jong church Sau remained on his knees for prayer. He listened to the warnings of those who had escaped from Da Mur, then prayed, and all but the most frightened in the church prayed with him. He finished, and rose to his feet. In the dim light of a lamp his face appeared troubled, his shoulders stooped.

"Go to your houses," he said. "Go quickly and pray. Pray for the people of Da Mur—and pray for yourselves."

The crowded church soon emptied. All moved to their homes with unusual quiet. There were no flares. Reaching home, the fires they had banked were now put out.

Sau spoke a few words to his brother, then started for Jong Lo. It had been a long day . . .

Kar, now alone in the church, prayed for several minutes, then blew out the lamp and carried it to his house.

His children slept. Gien was on her knees beside the big wooden platform that served as their bed. Kar slipped past his wife, careful not to disturb her prayer; he knelt by the table on which they ate their meals and stretched out his arms on the top.

In the black night he prayed—it must have been for an hour. He heard his wife get into bed. He prayed some more. He kept on praying, perhaps for another hour.

"God of Heaven," Kar pleaded, half aloud. He lifted his face skyward, opened wide his eyes as if to look through the thatch of his roof and up to the presence of God. "Let God make God's people strong, and give them assurance that God is their very present help—"

He did not finish. Suddenly he was dazzled by a light. It flooded the whole house, this brilliant light, and spilled into every corner. Not a flash, not a streak or ray, but a sustained, pervading light. By it he saw the sleeping forms of his family and the face of the watch he wore on a wrist. The watch hands pointed almost to midnight. Then as suddenly as it had come, the light went out.

He ran to a window. He could see nothing but solid blackness. He ran to the doorway and stepped out on the veranda. There was no moon nor stars. No flash of lightning illumined the sky. No fires glowed in any of the houses. Nor could he even make out the silhouette of the church only a short distance away.

Going back inside, he called to his wife. She answered, as she was only half asleep.

"Did you see a bright light?" he asked.

"A light? I thought I saw one," she replied sleepily, "but I wasn't sure."

"There *was* a light," he said. "I don't know what it was. Go back to sleep."

Yes, she could sleep. She could rest peacefully.

"Sleep soundly," he said, and there was a happy ring to his voice.

Kar crossed the floor to the table. Sitting, he prayed again. He prayed until he fell asleep. And as he slept he dreamed that a light shone from Heaven upon their valley. In the villages it was as if the sun shone at noon. But outside, where the jungle men watched from hiding places, all was the blackest of black nights.

14

"If God Wants Me to Live"

Brother . . . brother . . ."

Kar awakened quickly and crossed to the doorway. The stars shone now, and by their light he could make out the figure of a deacon of his church who stood at the bottom of the notched pole.

"Come in," Kar said. The deacon was panting, but being a nimble man, he scampered up. Kar led him to the table. They spoke in whispers.

"I had to come in the night," the deacon said, not waiting to catch his breath. A considerate man, he apologized for breaking into Kar's rest.

"It is all right, uncle," Kar replied. "What brings you?"

"The Viet Cong."

"What about them?"

"They are going to kill Sau!"

"How do you know?" Kar asked. He had heard someone say this in the confusion at the church last evening, but the deacon spoke as if he were sure.

"A remnant of the jungle men linger at Da Mur," the deacon answered. "As I stood among the trees, I heard them plotting. They intend to kill your brother by slow torture. Ha Rong has vowed it."

"Ha Rong!" An expression of astonishment crossed Kar's face.

"He is one of them now."

"This I heard from the ones who escaped Da Mur," said Kar, "but I could not believe it."

"Believe it, my pastor. He has sworn to come here to draw Sau's blood."

"My brother is not here," Kar said.

"They believe he is. They know he spoke last evening in our church."

191

"He took the path to his own home."

There was no moon, so in the shrouded house Kar could hardly see the one who sat opposite. The deacon, though, reached across the table to grip Kar's arm, giving emphasis to what he was saying.

"Then they will go to Jong Lo to seek him out." The deacon pushed back the bench on which he sat. "I must leave to warn him."

Kar stood up with the deacon. He said, "My brother must flee. When you find him, tell him Kar said it."

"But, you—should you not also flee?" asked the deacon. He was now concerned for his own pastor.

"No," said Kar. "It is not I they want.".

"But you are a pastor."

"Sau is our leader," Kar replied. "He brought us to this place away beyond the reach of the Viet Cong in the mountains."

"But you are his brother!"

"I am," Kar said calmly, "but my place is here with my people. Of this, God has assured me." He paused, then continued. "With Sau it is different. The God-Followers of a vast area look to him as their leader. They need the inspiration that he has brought—the teaching, the fatherly comforting." Kar uttered a reflective sigh.

"Some must move up and down the land to care for many churches," he said. "Others must stay with one people. God sent me and my wife to the Tring, and with the Tring we will stay until we die."

They had walked to the veranda. Kar bent his tall frame to speak directly into the man's ear. "Many months ago the jungle men marked my brother for death."

"This is no spur-of-the-moment scheme they plot?" the deacon asked.

"Perhaps with Ha Rong. Not with others."

"He is in danger wherever he goes?"

"Everywhere," replied Kar. "But now especially here. Go find my brother. He must not die needlessly."

As the deacon scrambled down the pole, Kar called softly after him. "Remind him that his house in Heaven is not yet finished!"

Kar went back to the table. He sat pondering this strangest of nights until the first pink streaks of dawn crept into the sky. From under the house the cocks crowed their greeting to the new day. Suddenly, Kar's ear picked up a rustling in the underbrush and the pad of a footfall outside. He stepped quickly out on the veranda to see who might be moving about in the semidarkness without announcing himself.

There, with his foot planted on the bottom step of the notched pole, stood Ha Rong.

From the veranda Kar looked directly down on him. The muzzle of a carbine, slung over one shoulder, pointed in Kar's direction. And in the breaking light of morning he met Ha Rong's gaze.

How long they stood there—Kar above looking down, Ha Rong below looking up—Kar did not know. It must have been the briefest of moments, yet it seemed more like years.

Ha Rong started to climb the pole, then paused, stopped by the soul-searching look of one who had taught him much. Whatever evil Ha Rong had intended to inflict was now thwarted by that look. He averted his gaze from Kar's, breaking the spell.

"No . . ." he groaned. "Don't look at me." It was as if he were speaking to God, not Kar, asking God to take His eyes off him, to stop probing the hearts of sinful men.

"Forgive me!" he cried, and fleetingly glanced up again at Kar. With this he dropped to the ground, turned, and ran until the forest swallowed him.

He had asked forgiveness. At that moment he had wanted it. But an hour later? A day later? A year? If he met Sau—

With Ha Rong, who could tell?

Sau sat in his house listening to Kar's deacon, who had awakened him before dawn.

"Ha Rong has sworn to take you—I heard him plotting," the deacon gasped. "And if he fails, a dozen of his evil comrades have pledged to cut your body apart."

"I know," Sau said quietly.

"You know?" The deacon was surprised.

"Men came across the log bridge from Da Mham to tell me," Sau explained. "Gai and Jieng and Mang have already been taken from there. Perhaps if they take me they will be satisfied."

"Is a hungry elephant satisfied with a single sapling, or even three?" asked the deacon. He drew near Sau. With a pained look, he cried, "I beg you to flee before the full light of morning comes!"

Sau sat without moving. He replied:

"The messengers from Da Mham said the jungle men would come to my village on Sunday. Today is only Saturday. I must preach tonight. After that I will go—if I go."

"But Ha Rong has vowed that today he will take you. I heard him say it myself." The deacon looked at Sau beseechingly. "You kept the people serving God instead of serving the enemy," he said. "For this they have condemned you."

"If God wants me to live, God can keep me from dying," Sau said.

"But your house in Heaven—Kar said to remind you it is not yet finished."

"Perhaps it is not," Sau said, and he smiled a little. "Tell my brother I will do the will of God."

Sau had not made up his mind to go. There was more to say to God. Although he had prayed the night through, he was not at the end of his praying. Therefore, when the deacon left, he climbed atop the wide wooden platform where his wife, a son, and three young daughters slept, and in the dimness of the house, he talked to God about Ha Rong.

"He lusts for things and for power," Sau said in his prayer. "When his wife was healed he was not grateful. He has sided with the jungle men. But he isn't for them as much as he is against God. He runs with the guerrillas. He is also running away from God."

Sau arose, his prayer ended.

He wondered where Ha Rong might be. Was he outside the house, ready to kill him by a bullet or an arrow? Or was he hidden just off the path in the forest, waiting his chance to spear Sau, or to club him into submission so he could be dragged to some remote spot in the jungle to be slaughtered there as drunken tribesmen slaughtered their sacrificial animals?

Sau tried to stop the shaking of his hands. He said to himself that he could not leave the village. He could not leave his house, or even the platform on which he was kneeling.

He was afraid. Here on this bed was his only security. No one could spear him from beneath so long as he stayed on his bed.

A ray of sunlight came through the weave of a wall. With his eye Sau followed the light from the tiny holes to a table. His Bible lay there, and seeing it, he gradually stopped shaking. There was where his security rested, in the Word of God—and in the Spirit of God dwelling within him.

He got up, crossed to the table, and opened the Bible. He thumbed the pages until he found one of the letters Paul had written to Timothy.

"For God hath not given us the spirit of fear," Sau read, "but of power, and of love, and of a sound mind."

Not the spirit of fear. He was ashamed for having been afraid. Within him was God's Spirit, and it was not the spirit of fear.

He thought, too, of a verse he had learned from K'Sol: "Greater is he that is in you than he that is in the world." This verse gave him courage to stand for God during the early days he had to stand alone. And this verse, along with others that were coming to him now, were pumping new courage into him.

As he meditated, Drim got up and went out of the house to collect firewood. Soon she came back. Sau took the load, and laying it next to the clay box, blew on the near-dead embers of the night's fire.

"I must go away," he said to his wife gently. He did not have to explain why he was going. She knew that with jungle men about he must leave the valley for the sake of his life. The parting would be hard, but she wanted him to go.

Although she would be alone with the young children, she was always willing to stay behind when his ministry called him on long and dangerous trips.

"You must go," she said. "This time as much as any other you are called to God's work."

The children had awakened—a son of ten years, and the three younger girls. The two older sons lived in Dalat. Sep, the unruly one, seemed to have settled down somewhat; he was being trained as a nurse in a government school. Nga, the second son since the beloved Roi had died, was going to school at the tribes center.

Sau gathered his smaller children around him.

"I will go to Dalat," he said, "although it will take a long time to get there because I must travel off the trails. There I will see Sep and Nga." To be with his sons was a pleasant prospect in an otherwise wearying undertaking.

Set, his only son at home, then asked to go with him. At first Sau said no, but finally consented.

Before leaving, Sau looked at his gun on the wall and at the few shells in a box on a rafter. Then without lifting the weapon from its place, he decided to go without it.

"The basket will be enough to carry," he said to Drim. "Where I am going there will be no pigs in a cornfield to shoot."

Drim and the girls followed Sau and Set onto the veranda and down the notched pole. As Sau lifted the basket to his back a man also bearing a light load walked from a nearby house. It was Poh, the fever-ridden pastor of Da Mur.

"I will go with you," he said. "Only the *moi lo* in Dalat can drive away my fever."

How had Poh known that he was going? Sau wondered. How had word got about that Sau was leaving for Dalat? Maybe someone had walked under the house as the family talked. However it happened, word of Sau's plans had spread; at least it had gone as far as the house where Poh stayed.

Who knew if it had gone farther?

Sau welcomed having another companion. He fished under his veranda for his walking stick. Then he strode to the edge of the forest with Poh and Set, and taking no path at all, stepped out of the morning sun into the dark green brush.

He turned for an instant. His wife and daughters saw him wave farewell. They saw the white of his teeth as he smiled. Then he was gone.

15

No Rain Like This

THE TERROR OF NIGHT did not vanish with the dawn for the inhabitants of Thach Trai. That morning five armed guerrillas bounced across the monkey bridge from deserted Da Mur to Sim Jong. It was time, their leader had decided, to take over another village.

As in Da Mur, the invaders routed the people from their houses and herded them together here, in the dirt street that ran through the center of the village. They alternately threatened or cajoled, using every trick to try to persuade the inhabitants to join the Viet Cong.

"Go with us into the forest so that our leaders can teach you!" one of the black-clad jungle men cried. Then someone tried another tactic. But the people remained adamant.

The guerrillas made one last attempt.

"If you help us in our fight we will let you keep your fields and herds and houses," they promised. The villagers remained stonily silent.

The guerrillas then warned them that they would be marched away at gunpoint. The people of Sim Jong only shrugged.

The villagers here seemed unafraid. Perhaps they got their boldness from their pastor Kar, who talked in a straightforward way to the rebels.

"You say you are strong," Kar said in reply to one of their speeches. "Well, our God is stronger than all the men of the earth."

Kar was unafraid in this hour because of the shining light. In the darkness of midnight it had seemed God's promise of protection. Kar stood firmly on his belief that all would be well in their village. For that reason he dared to be bold, and his bravery surpassed the boldness of the guerrillas. Getting nowhere, the five who had come on what they thought was an easy mission withdrew without harming a person in Sim Jong, and made their way one at a time across the monkey bridge.

"We will come back," they threatened. "Our chief will come with us. We will show you that the God of Heaven does not protect you."

Was this not the very warning they had left at Da Mur the afternoon before?

They departed. Kar breathed a sigh of relief. His people had not been harmed. All had gone well. All would go well. Yet, he realized that in each village the situation was grave.

On Sunday the jungle men struck at Da Rom. The invasion of the village, the rounding up of the people, the haranguing, were the same as elsewhere. But here there was one difference. At gunpoint they forced the Roglai to tear down their government house piece by piece. Once more they withdrew without inflicting an injury. The pattern seemed clear—first to menace, then suddenly to carry off the populace, then to return to loot.

By Sunday evening a rumor ran through all the settlements. Government troops and the Viet Cong had fought bloody skirmishes along the road from Thach Trai to the coast. When the fighting ceased the guerrillas had spiked and mined long sections of the road. Not even their own forces could use it now.

Later that night the deacon reported to Kar that he had seen two fresh graves at the edge of Da Mur.

"We believe they hold the bodies of Gai and Jieng," he said sadly. "We found Gai's broken watch on top of the dirt. We do not know the fate of Mang."

Another came to say that although he had not seen the killing, he heard about it from his old mother. She had been gathering herbs just after sunrise when she almost stumbled onto the scene of execution.

"Gai they hit with a shoulder ax," she reported. "Then I saw two men rush upon the two prisoners and stab them over and over with knives."

Before long the guerrillas left the valley. But in the days that followed a heavy air of uncertainty still lay over the four remaining villages. The people knew they had left, but did not know how far they had gone nor how long they would stay away.

Kar sent scouts into the forest—not to engage the jungle men in any sort of encounter, but to keep an eye on them, to try to learn of their plans, and to see if they could find any trace of the missing from Da Mur.

Upon their return these scouts reported to Kar that they could find no sign of the guerrillas. The jungle men had pulled back into the mountains, evidently taking the captives with them.

"Rest a day, then start the search again," Kar said. "For our own sakes we must be constantly on the alert."

Kar kept a watch posted in the surrounding forest. But since there was no indication of activity, the people of Thach Trai sought to turn their minds away from the horror they had known.

For over a month now the Viet Cong had been gone. In this time the calm that pervaded the villages of the God-Followers began to extend to some of the surrounding pagan settlements; here and there one or another forsook his fears—fear of the spirits and fear of the enemy—for a reassuring faith in the God of Heaven.

This was almost the end of November. In preparation for Christmas the pastors drilled the children and youth in music that would tell once again to their pagan guests from the villages around them the happy story of Christ's birthday. Kar appeared to have regained his good humor. He brought out his set of gongs, distributing the various-sized disks to willing players; he organized the people for many kinds of games. Gradually, the women ventured farther out among the trees to pick up firewood; the men walked to their fields to admire the biggest crop ever.

Life went on—but no one really believed it could go on this way for very long. There was the constant speculation, "Where are the jungle men now? When will they come again?"

But if there was uneasiness, it was still far from the paralyzing fear that had gripped them in the days of spirit worship. In the evenings, as the God-Followers met in their churches to sing hymns, to pray, and to hear the teaching of their pastors, they found they still enjoyed an inner peace that made them want to sing.

The wet monsoon was early this year. It came shortly before the rice harvest was ready for cutting. Without warning, the rain began to beat down savagely on the valley. It was quite unlike the usual start of the rainy months.

The downpour persisted. Except for men on sentry duty, the people stayed in their houses. On the fourth day Kar grew fidgety; he looked repeatedly at the big, colored calendar on the wall, as he had done almost hourly since the storm began to make sure he had the weeks straight. Yes, he had faithfully crossed the numbers off each day; the date today was November 27, 1960.

How odd, this rain! It might have been a typhoon strayed in from the sea, except there was little wind. Most of the time the rain fell straight down in heavy, chilling sheets. Kar hoped it would not spoil the crops.

Because of the rain, the vegetable bin was empty. Kar decided to take Gien's basket and venture out—rain or no rain—to pick some squash for their supper.

He put on a heavy rubber raincoat he had bought in Dalat, pulled on a pair of boots, and left the house.

The raincoat did not give him much protection. The water ran down his neck and into his boots; he decided the squash could wait. But why not have a look at the river before he returned to the house? Sloshing through the mud to a ridge that hid the river from Sim Jong, he was able to see the angry waters. The swollen stream was already high. If the rain continued, by tomorrow the river would be over the floor of the monkey bridge. Then, to get across, the people would have to use the utmost caution. Anyone who slipped into the surging current would be shot downstream at breakneck speed and dashed against the jagged rocks.

"I've not seen the rain come like this before," Kar thought to himself with concern.

As he turned away from the ridge, he saw someone in a great hurry bouncing across the planks of the monkey bridge. Kar recognized him as one of the scouts who had been in the jungle for several days on the lookout for guerrilla movements. As the man drew near, Kar noticed his expression of anxiety.

"Uncle!" the man cried. "Uncle, I just met two of the jungle men!"

Kar grasped the youth's cold, bare arm.

"You've run far to bring this word."

"They are coming tomorrow!" The boy's breathing was labored; he was overcome by a spasm of coughing.

Kar took him home; there, where it was warm and snug, he and the young sentry peeled off their wet clothes and exchanged them for blankets, drying themselves over a briskly burning fire. Gien, mindful of the chilling dampness, pressed hot cups of tea on them, and the tea warmed both their throats and their hands. Kar sent his children to far corners of the house to study their lessons. Turning to the youth, he asked him in a low voice what he had seen and heard.

The boy leaned forward.

"They were Chil—people of your tribe, but not of the Chil villages we know," he said. "They did not know me, so they answered all the questions I asked."

"They told you that men are coming here?" Kar inquired.

"They boasted that many men would be here tomorrow, as soon as the dawn first shows in the sky."

"They will come in the rain?"

"It was not raining up there where we were. But they care nothing for rain."

"What is the purpose of their visit this time?"

The youth thought a minute before answering.

"I will repeat to you their exact words. I do not want to make any mistake. They are coming to 'cut off the heads of the Big Chickens who do all the crowing'—those are the words the two tribesmen used."

Kar understood only too well the meaning conveyed by this homely manner of speaking. The "Big Chickens," of course, were those who led the people—he, Doi, and the other pastors. Their "crowing" was their preaching and teaching. *Kill off the cocks and the flock can then be stolen.* This was an old peasant adage. The jungle men would follow it. Kill Kar and Doi and Sieng and Jao, then lead the people away as they had marched off the leaderless ones of Da Mur.

Kar put on dry clothes; the youth lay on the big wooden bed to sleep off his fatigue. Gien drew to the fire's edge and there talked with her husband over more cups of warm tea.

"Will they come?" she asked.

"They will come," Kar said grimly. The two were quiet. Kar then spoke. "They will come as they came back to Da Mur, the smiles gone, the guns loaded."

"Will they take our people away?" she asked.

"The people of Da Mur were without a leader," he replied, pushing a piece of wood farther into the fire. "The people in the villages which remain have their pastors."

"But they will kill the Big Chickens first," Gien reminded him.

Their youngest child had awakened and was starting to cry.

"That is their plan," Kar admitted, as Gien got up to bring the infant, only a few days old, from the platform bed. "But we must remember—the light."

Kar stared into the fire. He was thinking about Sau, wondering where he was and whether he was in danger.

The young messenger had said the guerrillas named Kar and Doi as the two very biggest chickens—not Sau and Kar. What did that mean? Had Sau been discovered on his journey through the forest? Kar shuddered as he thought of the decree of the rebel court and Ha Rong's oath that Sau, if caught, would be tortured first, then killed.

In taking the people of Da Mur the jungle men had moved against a whole village; in the condemnation of Sau and the murdering of Gai and Jieng they had acted against individuals. Now their intentions portended ill both for the leaders and the people. "The Big Chickens who do all the crowing." Yes, he was certainly one of them himself.

"What will you do?" asked Gien, as though reading his thoughts.

"Do?" He was surprised at her question. "I will stay with our people."

He regarded his wife with tenderness.

"One day I told Sau that God had called me to teach the Tring. You came with me, and on our journey we arrived at a rock that neither of us could climb over. But God wanted us among the Tring, and God got us over that rock. We stayed as long as the Tring stayed and we came to this valley when the Tring came. God sent others to other people, but we'll stay with our Tring."

Where, indeed, could anyone go? Poisoned spikes of bamboo sealed off the road. The flooding river grew more treacherous by the hour. The well-armed guerrilla forces no doubt were encamped at that very minute across the river in the trails that led up into the mountains—mountains that once had been their home.

There was nothing more to be done. Kar could only wait to see what would happen as the people also anxiously waited. After supper that night he was able to sing with his children; he was able to tell them that God had given him assurance that everyone would be all right.

The people of the Thach Trai valley went to bed to spend an uneasy night. The unknown would arrive with the dawn.

Kar was awakened twice by the hard-driving rain. Each time he drifted back into fitful sleep. A third time he roused and heard no pounding, no splashing, no rivulets cascading to the river.

He listened to the sounds close by. They were the occasional ruffling of a chicken's wings under the house and the breathing of his wife and children asleep on the platform bed, the uncertain rhythm mingling with the cadence of the convulsive river.

Then a blasting sound broke open the night. Crashing, crunching noises followed in rapid succession.

Kar sat bolt upright. A child awakened and cried. Gien sat up.

Kar was off the bed and onto the veranda. Other householders spilled out also. The crunching noises came from behind the ridge.

"The bridge!" Kar shouted. "The bridge has given way!"

"The bridge! The bridge!" The people shouted the news from veranda to veranda.

The raging river had claimed it. Kar could picture at this moment the current making mockery of man's handiwork as it swept the spindly sticks of bamboo toward the sea.

Within an hour, just as dawn came to the valley, the villagers heard another boom, deeper this time, muffled and far off. They did not need to be told that the log bridge downstream at Jong Lo had also gone out.

In the growing light Kar smiled and bowed his head in thankfulness. He thought of the tributary between now deserted Da Mur and the people remaining in Da Mham. A roaring torrent would be pouring through there. He thought of the monkey bridge over which the guerrillas had come on their last visit. No chance of repeating their surprise today. He thought of the road so thoroughly spiked and mined. He thought of the swamps beside it.

The people of Thach Trai were sealed in their villages. There was no way for them to get out.

But at the same time there was no way for an enemy to get in.

16

The People's Decision

THE PEOPLE of Thach Trai slept little that night.

When morning came, they climbed up through the sticky mud to the ridge that lay between their homes and the river. There they looked out to see if their eyes would confirm what their ears had already told them.

Kar was not surprised that the monkey bridge had vanished. Between two banks was now an empty expanse of brown water, wide as a lake, deceptively smooth. Only the uprooted trees, bobbing and twisting along on the surface, revealed the speed of the waters in their headlong rush to the sea.

"Think of it!" Kar murmured to a villager standing beside him. "Not a stick left! Why hadn't we thought of demolishing the bridge to protect ourselves from enemy attack?"

But the God of Heaven had sent the rain. And now, that job done, the sun coming up with its usual brightness painted a sky of pink feathers.

Kar was still chatting with his people when he thought he noticed an unnatural movement in the underbrush on the far side of the water.

Instinctively, he clutched the arm of the man standing nearest him. "Look!" he said.

Even as he spoke, squat, stocky figures began to emerge and make their way toward the riverbank.

"It's the jungle men!"

"The Viet Cong!"

"They've come to make good their threat!"

An endless stream of men in uniform was pouring out of the forest to form a ragged line along the water's edge.

From their vantage point on the ridge not high above the widened river, the residents of Sim Jong stared fixedly at the intruders, separated from them by no more than a hundred meters of rushing water.

"How many are there?" a woman's voice asked anxiously.

"More than have ever come before," said Kar quickly. "Two hundred at the very least."

"They have guns!" another voice cried out.

Kar saw that they were within easy range. A volley fired into the massed villagers could have dreadful consequences. With a few crisp commands, Kar ordered them down from the ridge. He and a few others remained.

But the guerrillas did not shoot. Instead, they ran haphazardly up and down the banks like excited ants, evidently looking for a rock, a fallen log, a shallow ford, some place where they might cross. Having found none, they withdrew.

"They appear to be carrying out their plan," Kar mused as he watched them melt back into the underbrush. "They intend to kill only the Big Chickens that do all the crowing. Then, so they think, they can easily control the others. But for the time being, we're safe —at least for a little while."

No one would be able to get across that river today—or even tomorrow. But the day after? Or the day after that?

When he returned to show Gien the swollen waters, he noticed that the river had already receded by half a meter.

That evening as soon as it was dark, a small knot of villagers gathered warily behind the Sim Jong church. They conferred together in whispers. Later that night, by twos and threes they visited Kar's house for guarded conversations. Always they looked behind them. One never knew when another Ha Rong, another betrayer, might be lurking nearby.

The next evening they came again. This time the deacon and another older man of the village were sitting with Kar at his table.

"The jungle men have not departed," the deacon said. "We know this because we looked across today and saw them moving about."

"Who knows?" said the other man nervously. "Some may have reached our side of the river before the waters rose."

"Or they may be out in the forest building rafts," said Kar. "Within a few days the river will have dropped so that it will be an easy matter to pole across."

The deacon leaned forward.

"We must be gone before they come."

Kar drummed on the table with his fingertips.

"But how? By the road?"

"Not by the road," the other said. "The road is filled with spikes."

"How then?"

"By the river," said the deacon.

"There is nothing on which to travel," said Kar. "The rafts we once had were washed away."

The deacon was not to be so easily put off.

"We'll make new ones, then. We'll all ride them to the sea."

Kar stared long and hard at the two men who were so willing to face such a risk.

"You are not Roglai," he reminded them. "The Tring and Chil have not grown up beside the river. We fish in it, but who except the Roglai swim well?"

"Why do we need to swim?" the deacon asked with a shrug. "We will stay on our rafts."

"But the children may fall into the water," Kar pursued. "Their mothers will be terrified."

"We will trust God to keep us afloat," answered the deacon.

"But where will you go? What will you do?" Kar demanded. "Have any of you thought about what awaits you at the end of such a journey?"

This time the deacon said nothing.

"Remember," Kar went on, following up his advantage, "you will be able to take with you on a raft no more than you can carry in one small basket—your Scripture and hymnbook, your gongs, and a few handfuls of corn or rice to sustain you. And this is true for every family. Do you people realize that?"

The deacon nodded.

"We know," he said.

"And are you aware of what you are leaving behind?" Kar asked. "The biggest crop any of you have ever seen—corn, rice, manioc, sugar cane, not to mention the delicious bananas which grow wild in the jungle.

"Then there are your household goods which you have bought and paid for with much labor—your lamps, your bowls, your mats and hangings, your hardwood beds—these things you will never see again."

"We have thought of that," the deacon said.

"Why is it, then, that you are willing to give up all these hard-won comforts and go down the river to face the unknown?"

Kar studied the deacon's face as the latter looked out over the housetops before replying. Kar thought back to the day when he had asked his people to leave the mountains and go with him to Thach Trai. It had not been hard then for him to ask them to go, nor for them to accept. They had only to turn their backs on fear and sadness, on cold, discomfort, and hunger.

Now they faced a difficult choice. They must give up the only real comfort and security they had ever known for one reason—and one reason only: to be free from the threats of the jungle men.

When the deacon turned his eyes on Kar again, he was smiling.

"We take with us the things of the spirit," he said, "our faith, our courage, our belief, our freedom from fear, our ability to be happy. These things," he ended solemnly, "occupy no room in a basket."

Kar could scarcely conceal his gratification. Yet he had one final test in mind.

"You understand," he said, "that you *can* stay if you choose."

The deacon appeared perplexed.

"How is that?"

"Perhaps you have forgotten that the jungle men want only to cut off the heads of the Big Chickens who do all the crowing."

The deacon regarded him curiously.

"You mean then that in that case the rest of us could live here peaceably?"

"Yes."

"In other words, all we need to do is to hand over our pastors," said the deacon, a note of sarcasm creeping into his voice. "Then the guerrillas would not only let us remain to enjoy our harvest. They might even allow us to sing in our churches—provided we did not let our worship of God interfere with what they wanted to teach us."

"That is correct."

In the light of the oil lamp Kar could see that the deacon was shocked. Kar said nothing; he had his answer. The deacon went on.

"Do you think that we would choose to betray our pastors or serve the God of Heaven only when a man with a gun allowed us to—all for a bellyful of rice and lamps and houses and hardwood beds?" Shaking with anger, he stood up to go.

"No, of course you wouldn't," Kar cut in. Gently, he restrained the deacon from leaving.

Kar reflected that at another time some of the people might have proved untrue—hadn't Ha Rong betrayed them all? Yet the ones who stood true—they had been tested. They would not stay here to enjoy even a little ease under the hand of the enemy.

"Perhaps," said the deacon a little later as he was about to go, "I should explain to you why we feel as we do. Once we thought that abundance was the sole source of our happiness—just as back in the mountains we thought that our cold and hunger were the sole causes of our sadness.

"Since we have been here at Thach Trai we have learned a valuable lesson. Here we have enjoyed abundance. But now that we must make our choice between loyalty to God and the valuing of things, we have come to realize that whether we have or have not, is no matter of great importance."

The deacon paused.

"Is that not the lesson that your brother Sau learned from his vision years ago when he stood in the doorway to Heaven?"

Kar nodded.

"But we have had no such vision. We could learn only from our experience. And now we think we have done so. This we know: It is not the things of the earth to which we must hold fast. Rather, we must cling to the God of Heaven."

For a moment Kar could not speak. Then he said:

"What is the wish of the people?"

"They wait only for a word from you."

This time Kar did not hesitate.

"Tell them to get ready to go."

In the next few days no unusual activity was evident. The villagers avoided congregating in large groups lest some faithless one among them betray their activities to the jungle men. Instead, a father and his oldest son would slip away into the forest together.

There they cut down large clumps of bamboo and bound into bundles about twenty stems, each as thick as one's arm and twice the height of a man. Then they lashed two bundles together, side by side, to form a raft.

On top they lay slats of split bamboo crosswise, lacing them into place as a flat and fairly tight platform. Here would sit a mother, a grannie, perhaps two or three children. A raft could hold no more than five. The passengers would clutch the edge of the platform to keep their balance as the poler, standing either forward or aft, guided the course of the low-riding float as it was driven downstream by the swirling water.

"Father, I'm scared!" a man could hear his child say even before the launching. Aside from their fear, passengers would suffer the discomfort of riding always in a cramped position. And in the sun the heat would be merciless. There was no time for rigging up overhead shelters as they had done sometimes before. For the rewards of escape they could forego such luxury.

When a family completed its raft, neighbors went into the forest to help carry it to the river. No one announced openly whether or not he and his family were leaving. Each evening, as darkness fell, an increasing number of houses failed to show the light of a fire; they were empty, the family gone. Some, however, were afraid to ride the river at this time when it was high and furious. Others delayed their departure, since the jungle men did not reappear when the river began to go down.

"Brother," said a man who followed Kar into the forest to help build the two rafts for the pastor's large family, "I won't be building mine today."

Kar looked at him in surprise.

"Why not?" he asked.

"The river will be easier to travel tomorrow," the man answered.

"Easier for you, but for the jungle men as well," Kar said.

The man had another reason for not going.

"I will try to harvest my rice first," he said.

"We have been given these days in which to flee," Kar told him. "Don't tempt God."

In Da Mham, across the swollen river, the people led by Sieng were cut off from this activity. But they soon realized what was happening on the other side. People from all the villages were now

o

saying secretly to their friends, "Meet me downriver—or above in Heaven."

Early one morning, five days after the bridges washed out, Kar, having completed his rafts, hid them under the trees on the riverbank. Then he went back to his house. He took his family to a nearby shed where he dug a deep hole and in it buried six large copper kettles, four earthen cooking pots, a number of rice bowls, knives, and two green glazed jars for tea and water. These were the fruits of bounteous crops. But as he filled the hole and stamped the dirt down well and spread the surplus under his house, he said to his wife and children:

"I never expect to see these things again."

He took his family to a pen beside the house.

"The goats and pigs," he said, "will be useful to others—as long as people are here. When the last ones leave, they can turn the animals into the forest."

Kar was ready to go. He picked up the woven basket which held the most precious of his belongings—his Bible, a couple of bags of parched corn for the journey, and his set of brass gongs—and gently nudged his family along the path to the river.

As he crossed the ridge and started down the other side, one house after another slipped from view. Soon his own disappeared. Then the church. At last only the bamboo cross atop the church remained in his sight. In a moment the cross, too, was swallowed up behind the ridge. A lump came to Kar's throat. He brushed a tear from his eye. Then, resolutely, Kar turned to face the river and the unknown to which it led.

Many villagers had already congregated at the water's edge. Besides the two dozen who were leaving this morning, and who already had their scant provisions loaded aboard their rafts, there were about a hundred others who stood about restlessly, awaiting Kar's arrival.

When he reached the riverbank, he pulled aside the branch of a tree which ordinarily would have been high above the water, but which now barely skimmed its surface. Behind it were his two bamboo rafts.

"But they're so small!" exclaimed Gien.

Just then one of their boys jumped onto the nearest raft and almost overturned it.

"Be careful!" Kar warned him. "When you are on the water,

you will do only what you are told, when you are told."

Kar helped Gien, who carried the baby strapped to her back, to a place on the farthest raft, and divided the eight children equally between the two floats. Settled in their places, the family waited expectantly. They were crowded, huddling in the small space, but the children particularly were excited at the prospect of adventure.

"Cut the line!" Kar called to his son. "Do it when I do."

Drawing his knife, with a flourish he slashed the vine that held his own float to the tree. A few seconds later his son did the same, almost losing his balance. Pushing against the bank with their long bamboo poles, the two of them shoved off. With his free hand Kar waved to the crowd.

"Good-by!" he called. "Come as soon as you can—before it is too late. God protect you in the meantime."

As he spoke he poled the raft out through the sluggish backwater. Suddenly it was caught up in the turbulent waters of the mainstream and catapulted forward on a swift, crazily zigzag course.

At the first opportunity, Kar looked anxiously over his shoulder to see how his oldest son was handling the raft with Gien and the other children aboard. He caught a glimpse of the slight figure, legs planted sturdily apart, now using the pole to guide the raft away from a looming rock, now using it to balance himself. Kar sighed with relief. The boy was going to be all right.

Far behind, a long line of other rafts bobbed along bearing other families, neighbors and friends. Kar breathed a silent prayer for their safety. The hours ahead would be hazardous. A raft could so easily founder in splinters on a rock or become entangled in the crown of a new-fallen tree. Or if one were to capsize, a whole family could easily drown before help reached them.

In spite of the dangers, the swiftness of the current had its advantages. Under normal conditions two full days or more were necessary to reach their objective—a point just short of Nha Trang where three rivers joined. But now they should be able to complete the journey in a day and a half or less.

During the first few hours Kar and the other polers had no time to think about anything else. But gradually they grew accustomed to handling their tricky crafts, so when they came to stretches where the river was more tranquil, they allowed themselves to think of other things.

New fears obsessed them. Whenever opportunity offered, they glanced nervously at the protecting foliage along the banks, ever alert for an unfamiliar movement or form that would indicate the presence of an enemy.

They felt constantly that they were being watched by hostile, unseen eyes. Then, about mid-afternoon, a poler not far behind Kar cried out:

"There in the shadows—quick! A man with a gun."

Kar glanced up for a split second. He dared not take his eyes from the river for very long. He could not say for sure whether the man was right or not. But it would appear that he was, for his cry was being echoed from other rafts back up the river.

After that, Kar scanned the bank when he could. But he saw nothing.

Suddenly, as his raft abruptly rounded a sharp turn, Kar saw on a bluff high above the water five armed men in black shirts and black trousers, standing motionless, stolid, as though carved from stone.

Kar fought against the panic that threatened to overwhelm him. He had an impulse to crouch, to hide, to seek protection from the guns pointed in his direction.

At the same time he knew there was no place to hide, no way to escape. His courage returned. It seemed as though God was telling him not to think but to act.

"Pay attention to the job at hand!" he said to himself half aloud. "Get your people safely past. That's enough for you to do now."

He turned his attention back to the river and just in time, for the channel had grown narrower again, the current swifter and more tricky. His task now was to remain steady and unperturbed, to indicate with a wave of his pole the presence of hidden boulders as a signal to those who followed. He was glad that it called for all his concentration and all his skill.

He had an eerie feeling that the sights of five menacing guns were trained on him. He was thankful for the bobbing, bouncing, twisting course of the speeding raft which at the moment made him a difficult target for any but the most expert marksman.

Just then a voice called out in peremptory command:

"You in the lead—pull in here! Pull in to the riverbank!"

From the corner of his eye Kar caught a glimpse of the man

waving his weapon to indicate the spot. Kar could hardly keep from laughing outright. In these swift waters it would have been impossible to comply with the comand, even if he'd had any intention of doing so.

He waited, almost expecting a shot to ring out. He heard none.

Kar felt a pair of tiny arms around one leg.

"Are they going to kill us?" A frightened voice begged an answer.

"No, son, no." The confidence with which he spoke brought reassurance to himself.

He wondered how many others were afraid at this moment as his son was afraid, as he himself had been afraid. He saw that the other rafts were coming now, approaching the stretch of fast water. But they were being guided steadily and with determination.

At last he could look ahead. About a hundred yards further on the river took another sharp turn. Once there, they would be out of range of gunfire. Length by length it drew near, until he could reasonably believe that he and his people would make it.

And if they did, what then? What would they find beyond?

17

Tall against the Sky

THEY REACHED THE BEND in safety, only to see there other armed guerrillas—sometimes one alone, sometimes two or three crouched together on the riverbank. Strangely, however, none tried to interfere with the people's flight.

When it grew so dark Kar could no longer see the snags ahead, he ran his raft up on a sandbar in the middle of the river. The others then beached theirs abruptly, dumping the riders out onto the sand.

"We'll camp here for the night," Kar said, helping women and children to their feet.

The weary travelers were glad to break their journey. But some, mindful of the threatening Viet Cong, had little appetite for the cold rice the women had brought; they doubted they would survive the night. No one made a fire. The expanse of river separating them from the shore would keep them safe from animals; they hoped the current would also protect them from any human foe. Eventually, the camp settled down; the sentries kept watch, but saw nothing.

Long before the sun rose, all were up again and ready to resume the journey. The second day's travel pitted them against the same natural enemies. But after they reached the coastal plain they came into an area that was controlled by government troops. From that point on they saw no more jungle men.

All through the morning of the second day, Kar kept scanning the river for the red-tiled roofs and tawny walls of an ancient fortress known as La Citadelle. This was to be the end of their journey, the point of rendezvous with those who had already made the trip. Loc, the district chief, maintained an office there, Kar knew.

It was almost noon when Kar, rounding a sharp bend in the river, saw the walled city looming ahead. From that point on, manipulating his pole with skill, he guided his craft toward the sandy bank, waving to the those behind to follow him. As he drew near for a landing, he saw a crowd on the shore waving wildly and shouting.

"You've come! You've come!" Men, women, and children on the bank cried excitedly. Others were hastening from a gate in the walled fortress. Word of the arrival had spread, and all the tribesmen at La Citadelle were running out to meet the newcomers.

"It's our people!" Kar was shouting now himself. In the joy of seeing alive those who had run the dangerous course before him, he almost lost his balance. His raft drew close enough that he could recognize faces. He saw many there who had come from Jong Lo. The pastor Jao was among them.

The reunion would have to wait, however, until each of the rafts was safely beached. This done, Kar and those who traveled with him exchanged warm greetings with the earlier arrivals.

"Is Sau here?" It was Kar's first question. He spoke urgently, looking around. One after another, they shook their heads.

"We have heard nothing."

"Not from Dalat or Nha Trang?"

Again they shook their heads. Kar fell silent, overcome by this great disappointment.

In a few moments he came across Drim in the commotion on the riverbank. He asked her if she had news of Sau. She did not.

"Have we escaped only to discover that my brother has been killed by the jungle men?" he asked, crestfallen.

Jao tried to get his attention. He was asking if Kar had encountered guerrillas during his flight. But only slowly did the shock of not meeting Sau wear off. It was some minutes before Kar began to join in the conversations of the jostling crowds around him.

Jao asked his question again.

"Yes," Kar replied, "we saw guerrillas." He explained how the current had swept them past the men with guns.

"God was with us, too," Jao said. There had been five rafts in Jao's group. One was dashed against a tree.

"We overturned," Jao related. "We were all thrown into the water, but none of us was drowned.

"As we pulled up to the bank to repair the damaged raft, a man suddenly stepped out of the forest. He asked what we were doing. We thought the end had come."

"One of the jungle men?" asked Kar.

Jao nodded. "He carried a gun, and shells around his waist."

Another who had been on the capsized raft heard Jao's account and joined the conversation.

"In the end," this one said, "the jungle man put down his gun and helped us repair the raft."

Someone suggested that the travelers must be weary. Several persons now came up to Kar to tell him that the district chief had given the tribespeople permission to make their temporary home in a large building within La Citadelle's walls. The refugees now numbered about three hundred, so already the building was crowded. But the people were glad enough to have a roof over their heads.

The newcomers were led through the gate into the fortress. The structure loaned by Loc was of tawny plaster, and big as a warehouse. Once a palace, its gilt and decoration had long been gone. Its walls were broken by several openings larger than doorways. Inside was one vast room. Families used their scanty blankets, not needed here for warmth, to curtain off areas for privacy.

A few days after Kar's arrival, Jao took him aside to express concern about the villagers who had not yet left the valley. Jao proposed that they form a party and return to Thach Trai by way of the road.

"We will help them build their rafts," he said to Kar, "so they can soon come to join us."

Kar knew that if the people still in the valley lingered too long, they might never be able to escape to freedom. A worried look clouded his face.

"How will you get past the bamboo spikes in the road?" he asked.

Jao remained unperturbed. This he had foreseen. Already he had arranged with Loc for a hundred soldiers of the Vietnamese army to go with them. Trained experts would remove the mines and spikes in their path. Others would protect the tribespeople from attack by the Viet Cong.

But Kar was still reluctant to give his approval.

"The current grows slower as the flood abates," Jao reminded him. "It is far easier to ride downstream now than in the days when we came."

"Yes, the current is slower," Kar said, nodding. "But it also makes the rafts easier targets for the men on the banks."

Kar was thinking of the risks that those here had already taken. He did not want one of them to lose his life now. But a serious food shortage was already threatening at La Citadelle. The small supplies the people had brought were nearly gone. He looked around the big old palace and the specter of families on the verge of starvation loomed before him.

A party going to Thach Trai would be able to bring with them on the return trip food from the valley's bounteous supply.

"Go ahead and choose your men," he said to Jao. "Bring back all the people. And make as much room on the rafts as you can for rice. We will need it."

Kar himself started building houses with the bamboo from the rafts. There was plenty of room on the sandy bank for a temporary village. As more people from the valley joined the refugees, every possible shelter would be in demand.

One day about a week before Christmas Kar and his helpers stopped work long enough to say good-by to a score of tribesmen led by Jao and more than a hundred soldiers. They were setting out for Thach Trai.

Kar stood before them to give his final instructions:

"It will take you two days by road to reach the valley. You will spend two more building rafts. You should make it downstream again in a day or so. You have plenty of time. We will expect you back by Christmas."

Then Kar went back to work on the hot sandy bank. How strange it still seemed to him to be the acknowledged leader! With Sau absent, it was he who had given the nod to leave the troubled valley. It was he who had approved the plan to speed up the evacuation. Now he was directing the construction of a village to provide shelter for the overflow from the old palace of La Citadelle.

But even as he worked, his mind was forever plagued by the uncertainty of his brother's fate.

One noon when the house builders had returned to La Citadelle for a meager noonday meal and siesta, they were startled to hear a child shout as if beside himself:

"Uncle is here! Uncle is here!"

Kar was eating at a table of men. He looked up. Over another's shoulder and through the doorway he thought he saw a head of black curls. It couldn't be—he wouldn't let himself believe it!

Nevertheless, he sprang from his bench and scurried to the open-

ing. He looked out into the glaring sunshine. His incredulity changed
to sudden joy. He uttered a sharp cry.

"My brother!"

Outside the old palace, sitting astride a bicycle and grinning from
ear to ear, was Sau.

"My brother!" Kar's voice rang out again.

In a moment meals and siestas were forgotten as the building
emptied and a happy mob pressed around Sau. From somewhere,
Drim and the children came running.

Here he was—husband, father, brother, leader—alive and safe,
miraculously in front of them all. Drim wept. Kar quickly breathed a
prayer of relief. Sau hugged his children tightly while trying to acknowledge every greeting.

Everyone talked at once. They tried to tell him all that had happened since the morning he left the village.

To the barrage of questions Sau simply answered that God had
directed him safely to Dalat during those frightful days. In the course
of his escape he stopped in a number of Roglai and Chil villages to
preach; but never once in the roundabout journey through the mountains did he encounter jungle men. On his last lap, he traveled from
Dalat by way of Nha Trang, to learn there where his people were
gathering. Borrowing a bicycle, he had come here at top speed.

Sau had many things to say to them, but he would wait until the
rescue party returned from upriver. Kar assured him they would be
here by Christmas Day or even Christmas Eve. What plans, Sau
wanted to know, had been made for a Christmas program?

Hardly any. But Sau took hold. While the house building continued
under Kar's direction, just as much effort went into practicing for a
program under Sau's guidance.

Christmas Eve arrived. A depressing silence hung over the old
palace. No one had yet appeared.

"They ought to be here by tomorrow for sure," Sau said with a
frown. But he ordered the program postponed.

Throughout Christmas Day the people anxiously watched the
river—in vain. The following day Sau said with finality, "The program must be held tonight whether they come or not."

Many times that day Sau left the walled fortress to peer up the
river. He saw nothing.

Then, just at sunset, as the last rays of orange light filtered through

a window of the old shelter to shine on those who were putting the
finishing touches on the costumes, Sau heard shouts. They came from
the direction of the river. At the moment he was stringing up a
blanket for a stage curtain; in his excitement he let it fall to the floor.
The first rafts from Thach Trai had arrived!

With the others he raced to the bank. As far as his eye could see
was an endless line of bamboo rafts. In rapid succession the polers
guided their craft to the sandy shore, discharged their human cargo,
and now and then a basket of rice.

At first Sau counted the rafts by the dozen, then by the score. By
nightfall the last had come. This was the biggest exodus of all. Altogether, during these happy evening hours four hundred rafts bearing
more than a thousand persons reached La Citadelle.

"We brought with us what we could," Jao said, pointing to the rice.

Sau beamed. He was filled with pride that his once languid understudy had showed so much initiative in this undertaking. The baskets
were filled with rice from the new crop. There had been no room for
anything else—just people and a little food.

"By day some of us made rafts while others harvested the fields,"
Jao recounted. No longer did the youth shut his eyes as if asleep
when he spoke. His black eyes sparkled with enthusiasm.

"The days back at Thach Trai were perilous," he said, still on edge
from the experience. "Every night the jungle men shot into our camp.
The soldiers with us returned the fire. We don't know about the guerrillas, but none of our people was hit."

There was a scurry of preparation as the women made ready a
hasty meal for the newcomers. It was late that night when the Christmas program got under way. But never had there been one more
memorable, one more to be cherished and remembered.

Palm fronds wrapped the pillars of the old building. The clearing
for the stage was draped halfway around by blankets. A lantern hanging from a rafter illumined the happy expressions on countless faces.

A choir of boys and girls marched in; their feet were bare, their
faces scrubbed, their clean white shirts and blouses stiffly starched,
and trousers and long black skirts embroidered to emphasize the season. Their songs were a reflection of the joy that brightened the dismal
old palace to its farthest wall.

Sau's fingers drummed on the bench on which he sat as he kept
time to the staccato rhythms of the chorus. His lips formed the words

as first a shy boy then an unruffled girl recited from memory the age-
old story of Christ's birth.

The children's part finished, the gongers came on. Young men who
only hours before had been chiefly concerned with the enemy now
produced from Kar's metal disks a rolling melody. Then Sau felt
moved to say "a few words."

"God has kept both you and me," he said. Everyone recalled that
last night of horror when he had spoken of God's ability to preserve
them.

"This place is protected," he continued. "God has brought us here.
We are finished with moving, except to go to a place that the government will assign us where we will build our village."

He explained that the days of tribal independence were ended.

"We must go where others send us, at a time decided for us," he
said. "We will build our new village the way the government
specifies."

It was a regimentation they had chosen, he said, in order to preserve the one liberty they cherished above all others—the liberty of a
free conscience to worship and serve the God of Heaven.

Still, they were not entirely free here from the threats of the Viet
Cong, who, by now, had also moved downriver. No guerrilla had
shown himself yet in this region—but the people would have to exercise the utmost care.

The new village would be surrounded by a fence. The bamboo
spikes once so hated by the people as a symbol of oppression would
be planted in a ditch encircling the village. Sau had been assured by
his friend Loc that the young men would be given guns and ammunition; day and night they would guard the village gate. If necessary,
armed details would accompany the men as they went outside the
village to start new fields again. No longer would the people be helpless against the enemy.

"Perhaps the day may come when we can return once more to
Thach Trai," Sau said wistfully. But he knew it would be a long, long
time before the valley would be free of the jungle men who now over-
ran it. He knew his people might never again enjoy the abundance
they had so briefly tasted there.

But what did that matter? Sometimes, he reflected, thinking back
over his own past, to gain the world was to lose one's soul.